SAFE *and Fun* Playgrounds

SAFE and Fun Playgrounds

A Handbook

Heather M. Olsen, EdD, Susan D. Hudson, PhD,
and Donna Thompson, PhD

www.redleafpress.org
800-423-8309

Published by Redleaf Press
10 Yorkton Court
St. Paul, MN 55117
www.redleafpress.org

First edition 2016
Cover design by Jim Handrigan
Cover photograph by Patrick Lane Photography/Corbis
Interior design by Dorie McClelland
Typeset in Minion Pro and Gill Sans
Interior photos on page 33 and 100 by Jim Handrigan
Printed in the United States of America
22 21 20 19 18 17 16 15   1 2 3 4 5 6 7 8

Library of Congress Cataloging-in-Publication Data
Olsen, Heather M.
  Safe and fun playgrounds : a handbook / Heather M. Olsen, Susan D. Hudson, Donna Thompson.
     pages cm
     ISBN 978-1-60554-460-1 (paperback)
1. Playgrounds--Safety measures. 2. Play environments--Safety measures. I. Hudson, Susan D. II. Thompson, Donna. III. Title.
  GV424.O47 2015
  796.06›8--dc23
                          2015017239

Printed on acid-free paper

This book is dedicated to my coauthors,

Dr. Donna Thompson and Dr. Susan Hudson,

for their legacy, tireless energy, commitment,

and dedication to SAFE playgrounds.

—Heather M. Olsen

Contents

Acknowledgments

This book is the culmination of twenty years of work in the area of safe and quality play areas and playgrounds. Many people have supported our professional and personal journeys, and we would like to acknowledge their contributions to our efforts and their continued encouragement through the years, for which we are extremely grateful.

We would like to express our sincere appreciation to many colleagues at the University of Northern Iowa (UNI). Individuals who have provided services include the following staff of the National Program for Playground Safety (NPPS): Brandy Smith, Amy Bentley, Donna Mokricky, Sharon Regenold, Dr. Mick Mack, Jane Clark, and Phyllis Boelts. We appreciate administrative support from UNI presidents Dr. Robert Koob, Dr. Benjamin Allen, and Dr. William Ruud; presidential assistant Dr. Pat Geadelmann; Mr. Ed Ebert; deans Dr. Tom Switzer, Dr. Jeffrey Cornett, Dr. William Callahan, and Dr. Dwight Watson; and Health, Physical Education, and Leisure Services (HPELS) directors Dr. Doris Corbett and Dr. Christopher Edginton. We value the energy and enthusiasm of our student leaders: Brittany Ballantine, Megan Barnes, Heather Buch, Hilary Iverson, Elizabeth Messerli, Chelsea Miller, Claudia Pumpuni, Perla Quintanilla, and Betsy Vander Weerdt. We greatly appreciate your contributions.

We wish to give special thanks to US Senator Tom Harkin, US Senator Chuck Grassley, and former US Congressman Jim Nussle, who assisted with the Federal Appropriations for NPPS. We also appreciate the support from former colleagues at the Centers for Disease Control and Prevention (CDC), particularly the injury prevention unit, including Dr. Jeffrey Sacks, Tim Groza, Dr. Julie Gilchrist, Kim Blindauer, Sandra Coulberson, and Dr. Christine Branche.

We also wish to thank individuals from the Consumer Product Safety Commission (CPSC), including former chair Dr. Khalisa Phillips, and Ann Brown, John Preston, Debbie Tinsworth, Joyce McDonald, George Sushinsky, and Hope

Johnson Nesteruk. We also thank Kathie Morgan and Len Morrissey from American Society for Testing and Materials (ASTM) International. Both associations have worked hard to increase children's safety at the national level. Further, we appreciate the work of the International Play Equipment Manufacturers Association (IPEMA), Safe Kids Worldwide, Peaceful Playgrounds, Boundless Playgrounds, and KaBOOM!

We are indebted to other individuals who have served as safety school instructors, including board members Dr. Lawrence Bruya and Jean Schappet; and Tim Ahern, Dr. Melinda Bossenmeyer, Dr. Louis Bowers, Scott Burton, Dr. Annie Clement, Earl Colella, Judy Finkelstein, Carl Gabbard, Dr. Karla Henderson, Walt Henderson, Al Jackson, Lyn Kalinowski, Ken Kutska, Sharon Mays, Angela Mickalide, Jane Moorman, Mike Moran, Bobby Newell, Tom Netusil, Kim Newman, Tom Norquist, Judy Payne, Ken Ritchie, Beth Roberts, Deb Sampson, Jeanne Sanders, Mario Schootman, Robert Shiffer, Dr. Eric Strickland, Jan Sutkus, Mark White, Fran Wallach, and Sue Wortham. Your advice through the years has been greatly appreciated. We would like to acknowledge the support received from the Mike, Judy, Andrew, and John Kidd family, who have continued to advocate for playground safety.

On a personal level, Heather Olsen wishes to thank her family: Ben, Lyle, Siri, Brinn, and Liam. Your continued support and encouragement keep me enthusiastic and passionate about life and my professional and personal goals. Ben, I am forever grateful for your energy, wisdom, patience, and support. Lyle, Siri, Brinn, and Liam, I can't express the appreciation I have for you helping me see the wonder and beauty of nature's little things. Smelling flowers, watching birds, investigating bugs, and playing outside has renewed me. Thanks for reminding me to stop and enjoy all living and nonliving essentials. I can't wait for more adventures with you!

Susan Hudson would like to thank Dr. Sarah Rich, who has helped support the efforts of NPPS throughout the years by traveling to over twenty-four different states for research projects, speaking before professional groups on behalf of NPPS, and providing insight for new and innovative projects to be undertaken by NPPS. As a colleague and friend of over thirty-four years, her help and friendship have provided professional and personal comfort.

Donna Thompson would like to thank Shirley Shogren for her professional insights as an elementary teacher for many years, insights that have added value to NPPS. Further, as a most important friend of over thirty-seven years, her assistance and friendship have given great personal satisfaction.

Introduction

Playgrounds and play areas have changed a lot in the past hundred years. Today, when an increasing number of children are spending more time engaging in sedentary indoor activity and less time in vigorous, playful activity, playgrounds and play areas are more important than ever. Your challenge is to plan, create, and maintain playgrounds that can engross and challenge children. This is no easy task, for school, park district, and early childhood education budgets are more strained than ever before; litigation as a way of solving problems is more common than ever; and the agencies, staff, parents, community members, and other people with investments in play areas for children are more varied and divided than in the past.

Whether you're an early childhood educator or student; a grade school teacher or principal; a family child care provider; an out-of-school-time program director; or a park district staff member; a church, mosque, or temple activities director; a military recreation specialist; or a concerned community member, *SAFE and Fun Playgrounds* is designed to help you move through the many details and stages of making safe yet challenging playgrounds and play areas a reality. This book offers you important topics to consider, numerous resources to utilize, ideas for making your playgrounds engaging, and templates for maintenance to ensure that your playgrounds are free of unsafe risk, whether you're starting from scratch or thinking about upgrading or modifying existing areas.

We can say these things with some confidence because the three of us have almost eighty years of combined professional experience in playground safety. We founded the National Program for Playground Safety (NPPS) in 1995 at the University of Northern Iowa (UNI) to share our expertise with people throughout North America, Europe, Asia, South America, and Africa.

SAFE Playgrounds

SAFE outdoor playgrounds offer children **challenges** while minimizing their risks. They do so by providing developmentally appropriate play opportunities and play structures. They are accessible to children of varying abilities, including children whose disabilities are covered by the Americans with Disabilities Act (ADA) (1990).

SAFE is an acronym that stands for the four components we identified with a panel of experts and analysis by the **US Consumer Product Safety Commission (CPSC)** during our first year with the NPPS. This handy acronym and its underlying concepts have been adopted by other organizations, agencies, and individuals throughout North America. *SAFE* stands for:

Supervision
Age-appropriate design
Fall-surfacing
Equipment maintenance

SAFE and Fun Playgrounds offers a brief, concise guide to the most up-to-date information on SAFE playgrounds and play areas. (For the sake of brevity, we use the term *playgrounds* from here on, although many of you will be reading *SAFE and Fun Playgrounds* because you're concerned with *play areas*.) The book begins with a brief overview of the history of playgrounds and play areas in the United States (chapter 1) and moves on to the four elements of SAFE playgrounds, including the crucial roles of supervision (chapter 2), age-appropriate design (chapter 3), fall surfacing (chapter 4), and equipment and its maintenance (chapter 5). Chapter 6 addresses underlying administrative structures (planning and policies). In each chapter, terms that may not be initially familiar to you are **bolded** at first use; definitions of these terms can be found in the glossary at the back of the book. For those of you who are early childhood education students, we also include discussion questions at the end of each chapter to help you deepen your understanding of playground design and safety. An abundance of appendices provides useful data, links to resources, and templates for maintenance checklists. To keep yourself current with changes in the information we cover in *SAFE and Fun Playgrounds*, please regularly check the NPPS website, http://playgroundsafety.org, for updates.

Chapter 1

A Brief History of American Playgrounds

There is scarcely a daylight hour when the small playground outside the West 7th Community Center in Saint Paul, Minnesota, isn't alive with people: children from toddlers through five- or six-year-olds crawl among the rubberized mazes of the permanent structures, seven- to thirteen-year-olds swing from ropes or pump furiously on the larger swings, while teenagers and adults watch from the park benches or help the smallest children enjoy the bucket swings. All of this activity takes place on a soothing, bouncy greensward as clipped and tidy as a putting green. It is only when you stride across the spongy surface and sit down on a swing yourself that you notice the tips of the grass below are suspiciously golden and worn, the ground a little *too* elastic. The entire playground, you suddenly realize, sits atop an artificial **fall surface**; the handsome green lawn is actually synthetic turf.

This beautifully designed and maintained playground also sits atop a more than century-old history of urban visions, school and park district policies, community resolutions, and state statutes, all designed to make children's outdoor playgrounds pleasurable, challenging, and safe.

Playgrounds like West 7th's evolved from much more bare-bones play yards created in the nineteenth century. Before eastern and midwestern towns swelled with newcomers and became cities, children mostly played in streets. Factory work and the expansion of cities into outlying districts brought streetcars, horse-drawn delivery vans and wagons, and then the first automobiles onto roadways, eliminating safe places for children to play. The Massachusetts mill town Northampton built the first supervised outdoor playground in the United States, at Round Hill School in 1825. Starting in 1885, Boston developed a series of *sandgarten,* or "sand gardens," for children. The sand gardens were based on German models (fig. 1.1) and located at the Parmenter Street Chapel in the immigrant neighborhood of Boston's North End. The sand gardens were immediate successes: that first summer,

Figure 1.1. Sand gardens were introduced in Boston in 1885. Based on German *sandgartens*, they were safe places for children to play once streets became busy with traffic. This photo was originally published in 1921 in *The Play Movement in the United States: A Study of Community Recreation.*

"children came there, dug in the sand with their little wooden shovels and made countless sand-pies, which were remade the next day with undismayed alacrity" (Miller and Robinson 1963, 90–91). The sand gardens were enlarged in following years and their volunteer staff replaced by paid matrons. By 1893, expansion had resulted in ten summer playgrounds overseen by a general superintendent (Knapp and Hartsoe 1979).

By the turn of the century, playgrounds for children had become a national movement. President Theodore Roosevelt, a political Progressive and an enthusiastic advocate for what he termed "the vigorous life," saw playgrounds as necessary to city children's health and well-being. He invited members of the newly formed Playground Association of America (PAA) to the White House in 1906, later stating:

City streets are unsatisfactory playgrounds for children because of the danger, because most good games are against the law, because they are too hot in summer, and because in crowded sections of the city they are apt to be schools of crime. Neither do small back yards nor ornamental grass plots meet the needs of any but the very small children. Older children who would play vigorous games must have places especially set aside for them; and since play is a fundamental need, playgrounds should be provided for every child as much as schools. This means that they must be distributed over the cities in such a way as to be within walking distance of every boy and girl, as most children cannot afford to pay carfare (Rudolph 1907).

After 1907, playgrounds shifted from open spaces in which children could amuse themselves to ones equipped with structures that children could play on: one of the first of these was built at Hull House, Chicago's settlement house for immigrant families, in 1894 (Mero 1908). Early playground equipment was built from steel and designed to build the upper-body strength that youngsters would need in the factories and stockyards of growing cities. Little attention was paid to the safety of such equipment and the ground beneath it; instead, the reformers who created early playgrounds focused on the desirability of playgrounds as refuges from far more dangerous city streets. (See fig. 1.2.)

Initially, playgrounds were mostly found in cities; country children led more physically vigorous lives and were not seen as needing shelter from roadways or built amusements, as they had undeveloped woods, streams, and ponds nearby, and nature was viewed as one of their teachers. When the concept of physical education began suffusing schools throughout the United States in the early twentieth century and undeveloped areas for play disappeared from streetcar suburbs, playgrounds and play equipment began making inroads in exurban schools and communities as well.

By the 1920s, play equipment had become commonplace in community parks and schoolyards. Traditional swings, slides, merry-go-rounds, jungle gyms, parallel bars and horizontal ladders, and seesaws (teeter-totters) stood atop hard-packed earth or macadam (figs. 1.3 and 1.4). Early playground equipment was often built to be very tall: swing sets, slides, and jungle gyms were considered better the higher they were (fig. 1.5). However, as data on playground injuries amassed in the 1920s, critics and playground professionals came to believe that the chief culprit in children's playground injuries was the height of equipment. **Guidelines** published by the Playground and Recreation Association of America (PRAA), *Play Areas: Their*

Figure 1.2. Jungle gym in Hull-House playground in front of Mary Crane Nursery. Wallace Kirkland (photographer), n.d. Jane Addams Hull-House Photographs, JAMC_0000_0296_1125, Special Collections, University of Illinois at Chicago Library.

Figure 1.3. A stride pole above a packed earth surface. "N.Y. Playground" ca. 1910–1915. George Grantham Bain Collection. Courtesy of the Library of Congress LC-BC-2802-10.

Figure 1.4. A merry-go-round with packed earth beneath it. "Playground" ca. 1918–1920. National Photo Company Collection. Courtesy of the Library of Congress LC-F8-4461.

Figure 1.5. An example of the "higher is better" principle from Minneapolis, ca. 1910. "Playground, possibly North Commons." MH5 9 MP4 1 p68. Photographs Negative Number: 80029. Used with permission from the Minnesota Historical Society.

Design and Equipment (1928), and the 1931 **standards** issued by the PRAA's successor, the National Recreation Association (which became the National Recreation and Park Association [NRPA] in 1965), addressed the height of playground equipment, recommending that slides be limited to 8 feet (2.4 m.) tall and swings for young children to 6 feet (1.8 m.) in height (NRA 1907; NRA 1931). These standards remained unchanged and unchallenged until 1978, when the (CPSC) asked the NRPA to assist in the development of safety standards for playground equipment. While these standards referred obliquely to falls by specifying **protective barriers** on 8–12-foot (2.4–3.7 m.) equipment, they did not address or seek to limit the height of the equipment itself (Knapp and Hartsoe 1979).

In many communities, these tall, early playground structures have never gone away. In others, they were supplanted in the 1970s by what Joe L. Frost (1992) terms "the novelty era in design," the period when climbing and play structures became sculptures of cement and wood. During this time, commercial playground manufacturers began producing climbable rockets, ponies, turtles, and other animal pieces. This era also saw the creation of nursery play yards and European-style adventure playgrounds, in which children could build their own structures and create things.

Figure 1.6. A composite structure that allows children continuous play by eliminating the need to move between play structures.

Such playgrounds, though often developmentally more appropriate to children than those equipped with traditional fixed structures, found few fans in the United States, for they looked junky and were difficult to supervise (Frost 1992).

A parallel development affecting the design of playgrounds occurred in the 1970s, much of it driven by academic research. For example, at the University of Illinois at Champaign, researchers noticed children spent more time moving between play structures than on them (Wade, Ellis, and Bohrer 1973). In response to this discovery, playground creators began building composite structures (fig. 1.6). The era's fondness for wood and plastic surfaces was mirrored in these new play structures; wooden decks with plastic or wooden play structures attached to them became available.

It is those 1970s playground structures, along with the even older steel ones, that have become the source of many parents' and grandparents' nostalgia and resistance to change. Older people fondly remember this play equipment—much of it now banned by the federal CPSC and the NRPA—often protesting its replacement with newer and safer equipment: "I played on that all my childhood, and I never saw anyone get hurt. Why isn't it good enough for kids anymore?"

Nostalgia conspicuously lacks historical perspective; those of us who played on and remember such equipment tenderly remember it in the way children remember things. In those far-off days, peers who were injured on such equipment simply disappeared until they healed, and parents did not sue schools or recreation districts or blog about their children's injuries. Because of these things, it is easy for those who survived such equipment to believe that no one ever became seriously hurt on it, although many children did. Even on today's safer equipment, the CPSC estimates more than 200,000 children each year suffer injuries on American playgrounds serious enough to require emergency treatment (O'Brien 2009). Fond memories, then, distort our views of the safety of the playground equipment we grew up with.

Social changes have helped make the old equipment more dangerous than it may have been initially. In the past, most children did not use playgrounds until they were old enough to walk or bicycle to them on their own. Today parents and caregivers take the tiniest toddlers to playgrounds, where the children may attempt to play on equipment intended for older children. Additionally, many of today's children are physically less hardy than their parents or grandparents at the same age. They are more likely to spend after-school hours on computers or playing video games than riding bicycles or climbing playground structures. With fewer or less developed gross-motor skills than earlier generations of children of the same age, children today need better protection on play equipment.

As a result of these shifts, in the 1980s, the CPSC and the American Association for Leisure and Recreation (AALR) Committee on Play began advocating for better-designed and better-equipped playgrounds. The CPSC published the first edition of its *Handbook for Public Playground Safety*, the first guidelines for public playgrounds, in 1981. Injury statistics were collected, and the results proved alarming: as playgrounds continued to proliferate, children were suffering an unprecedented number of major injuries.

Researchers looking at the developmental needs and skills of young children also made alarming discoveries: play was being undervalued, even in child care settings, in response to parents' insistence on early academic preparedness. Research also showed that the play equipment in many parks, schools, and ECE centers proved to be developmentally inappropriate for the children using it.

Sunnyside School is a typical midwestern elementary school in a town hit by hard economic times and declining test scores. A few years ago, its local board of education decided to pull out all of the old playground equipment and do away with recess. After all, as one school board member put it, "Play is simply not important in this competitive world!"

The same school board member was appalled nine months later when he saw the progress report for the school: not only had test scores declined further, but incidences of fighting, bullying, and other antisocial behavior had increased. Teachers wrote about the lack of energy, focus, and attention in their young pupils.

After serious discussions with parents, teachers, and community members, the school board voted to reinstate recess for the coming year and work with the local community foundation to develop a playground that would reinforce curriculum through informal play. The following year, encouraging improvement was seen—enough so that continual changes were made to improve the play areas. After three years, the transformation in student interactions, attention, and test scores was dramatic enough that the fourth "R"—reading, writing, arithmetic, and recess—became a permanent fixture in Sunnyside School's curriculum.

As US countryside disappeared into expanding suburbs throughout the 1990s and 2000s, advocates for childhood play began calling for playgrounds that could provide not only vigorous physical exercise but also open-ended explorations of the natural world. The result was a new kind of playground, the "natural play area," which uses native plants, fallen logs, boulders, water features, and other structures to help city and suburban children discover nature (fig. 1.7). The equipment in such playgrounds is often different from traditional playgrounds: nets, ropes, and other devices replace static structures to give children more dynamic experiences (fig.1.8).

These are exhilarating times for those of you who advocate for childhood play! The importance of play to children's emotional, intellectual, social, and physical well-being is increasingly recognized. Shifts in the ages and abilities of children

Figure 1.7. In natural play areas, traditional play equipment pieces are being transformed to blend into the natural surroundings, such as these slides being incorporated into the natural slope of this center's land, which enhances the feeling of playing in the outdoors.

Figure 1.8. Newer equipment provides children with a variety of learning experiences by offering them many different devices to use, such as sloped climbing walls, rope ladders, and slanted platforms.

using playgrounds are prompting greater attentiveness to the developmental appropriateness of play structures. City and suburban playgrounds are being rethought and refitted—or carefully planned and built for the first time. We will look next at the first element today's playgrounds need to make them **SAFE** for toddlers through school-age children: appropriate **supervision**.

Discussion Questions

1. Visit a nearby park, a grade school, and a child care facility to look at their playgrounds. Observe these playgrounds at the time of day and day of the week when you think plenty of children will be using each place. Determine what supervision is available at each site. Characterize the equipment you find there: Can you determine what ages of children the equipment is meant for? What era would you estimate the equipment comes from?

Chapter 2

SAFE Supervision

Do you remember the first time you sat unassisted at the top of a slide and looked down? The people below appeared unimaginably small and far away; your distance from the ground seemed almost giddily vast. Getting onto that chute and speeding down to the safety of the playground and your friends seemed like an immense step. If you can remember the first time you slid down on your own, or the first time you wobbled along the sidewalk on your new bike, you already know what catnip such physical and psychological **challenges** are to children. Ensuring that such challenges are **SAFE** is key to maintaining or creating a good playground.

There is a delicate dance among the four elements of SAFE playgrounds: all of them must be in play simultaneously. Effective **supervision** is what ties these elements together. This chapter addresses the first component of SAFE playgrounds—supervision—and describes the organizations that have developed **guidelines** and **standards** you can use in creating your own SAFE playground.

Supervision

Playground supervision should be active but unobtrusive (Hudson, Olsen, Thompson, and Bruya 2010). Supervisors should direct children to appropriate SAFE play structures and away from equipment that is unsafe for them to use. Supervisors' interventions are critical to saving lives, preventing injuries, avoiding litigation, and complying with standards of care (Thompson, Hudson, and Olsen 2007). When supervisor intervention doesn't happen, a tragedy may occur, as it did to a child named Josh.

Josh was an energetic six-year-old kindergartner whose favorite time during the school day was recess. On a sunny April day, Josh, as well as 148 other children in kindergarten and first grade, raced outside for afternoon recess. A twenty-year veteran teacher followed the children outside and then turned to line up eight of the children in a time-out for indoor misbehavior. An aide brought out four children with special needs and walked them to the far end of the playground.

Josh didn't notice any of this. He was intent on playing with a rubber playground ball, which kept eluding him because his hand-eye coordination was not well developed. When he bent over to retrieve the ball, Josh accidentally kicked it. The playground surface was asphalt, and the ball rolled away, with Josh in hot pursuit. The ball rolled past the orange cones intended to demarcate the playground and onto the four-lane highway that fronted the school. Chasing after the ball, Josh ran into oncoming traffic, which tragically ended his life. (Hudson, Olsen, Thompson, and Bruya 2010)

Josh's unnecessary death points to the intricate interplay among several SAFE factors: this school had assigned only two adults to supervise 149 children on the playground. The veteran teacher was focused on only eight of them; the aide was focused exclusively on another four. No one was watching Josh and the other 136 unsupervised children on the playground.

Other SAFE factors figured in Josh's untimely death too: the six-year-old's hand-eye coordination was atypical for a boy his age, making the lively rubber ball a developmentally inappropriate choice of toy for him. The surface of the playground was asphalt, so the ball could, and did, roll a long way after the inexperienced child failed to catch it. Additionally, the playground was not protected from the nearby highway by a fence, but only by orange cones, and the preoccupied child failed to notice—or perhaps did not understand—what the cones signified. Most components in the SAFE system were missing in this situation, but the most conspicuous absence was that of adequate supervision.

Although supervision is frequently invoked in educators' circles, little actual attention and training are devoted to it. In our many years of experience, we have seen that it is often overlooked as an important element in the care and education of young children. Early childhood programs are held responsible for quality care and teaching, because these things play critical roles in helping children develop physical, emotional, social, and intellectual skills. But children need safety and security before they can enjoy developmentally appropriate opportunities in outdoor settings, and training in supervision is usually scant.

Moral Dimensions of Supervision

Supervision is the moral responsibility of people charged with the well-being and productivity of others. Where children are concerned, supervision consists of monitoring their actions and environment and ensuring that the equipment they use is appropriate to their activities. In child care and school playgrounds, supervisors monitor children's play to ensure that the play itself is developmentally appropriate and that it occurs in or on well-maintained equipment and **fall surfaces**. One definition of play supervision stresses *attention* (watching and listening), *proximity* (how far the supervisor is from the supervised), and *continuity of attention and proximity* (constant, intermittent, or not at all) (Morrongiello and Schell 2010). Supervisors must synthesize complex information, including children's developmental stage; hazards present in the playground; and kinds of injuries children may incur (Saluja et al. 2004). In its recent health and safety standards, the American Academy of Pediatrics (AAP) notes, "Children like to test their skills and abilities. This is particularly noticeable around playground equipment. Even if the highest safety standards for playground layout, design and surfacing are met, serious injuries can happen if children are left unsupervised" (American Academy of Pediatrics 2011, 65).

Legal Dimensions of Supervision

Almost every lawsuit for **negligence** cites lack of or poor supervision (Dougherty et al. 1993; Van der Smissen 2007). Programs and individuals serving children are obligated to provide adequate supervision and can be found negligent if they do not properly do so.

In a lawsuit, if a "reasonable and prudent" person would think that children should not be left unsupervised in a certain situation, the grounds for negligence are usually met (Hudson and Abraham 2010). A negligence claim can arise, for example, when a staff member remains indoors, gathering activity supplies, while an accident occurs among unsupervised children on the playground. A "reasonable and prudent person" would understand that small children should not be left unsupervised; if this is the opinion of a judge or jury, the staff member's absence usually qualifies as negligence (Hudson and Abraham 2010).

An act of negligence occurs when a supervisor fails to act or acts unprofessionally. One common act not in accordance with the **standard of care** is a supervisor's lack of active monitoring. In a handful of cases, we have observed supervisors sitting on benches, completely disengaged from the children they are supposed to be monitoring. In the case of Josh's death, the twenty-year veteran teacher and the other supervisor focused their attention on a handful of children, leaving most of the children on the playground without supervision.

Four conditions must be met for a child care program, school district, or community agency to be found negligent:

- deviation from the duty of a supervisor
- an act that is not in accordance with the standard of care
- **proximate cause**, or a connection between damage or injury and failure to act properly
- injury or damages that result from failure to act properly

Let's look at each of these challenges to adequate supervision.

Duty of a Supervisor

Staff members of early childhood programs, owners of home care businesses, school districts, and community agencies have a legal duty to supervise the children in their care (Van der Smissen 2007). Staff and programs are liable for injuries and damages that occur when supervision is inadequate. Supervisors who fail to act or who act unprofessionally may be found guilty of negligence (Van der Smissen 1990). The veteran teacher who failed to watch her many charges on the playground supervised only the eight children she had lined up for a time-out; the aide attended only to her own four students. The school district was negligent because the teachers, who were its employees, did not adequately carry out the acts of supervisors.

Standard of Care

Courts determine the standard of care required of early childhood programs, school districts, and community parks. Those standards are usually based on the recognized professional practices of local and state programs; these, in turn, are often based on principles developed by the National Association for the Education of Young Children (NAEYC), the NRPA, the National AfterSchool Association (whose 2009 standards for quality school-age care include those for school-age care professionals), the National Education Association, and state and federal departments of education.

Proximate Cause of Damage or Injury

The actual cause of a damage or injury is known as the *proximate cause* (Van der Smissen 2007). Negligence is established when the damage or injury can be proven to be the direct result of a supervisor's actions. In the case of Josh's death, the veteran teacher and the aide failed to supervise the young boy and most of the other children, and Josh ran into the road and died. Lack of supervision constituted the proximate cause of his death.

Injury to a Person or Damage to Property

An extensive review of lawsuits involving playground activities (basketball, football, softball, baseball, and soccer) demonstrates that courts looked at the duties, acts, and standards of care of supervisors (Dougherty et al. 1993) when considering the proximate causes for injuries. In the case of Josh's death, inadequate supervision resulted in the boy's death.

Duties and Practices of Supervisors

The goal of playground supervision is to protect children. Achieving this goal involves planning, active monitoring, managing, and responding adequately to emergencies. Researchers examining the supervision provided by caregivers have recommended that supervisors assess the following:

- developmental stage of the children in their care
- hazards in the setting
- kinds of injuries to which children may be susceptible
  (Saluja et al., 2004)

Active Monitoring

Good playground supervisors are similar to lifeguards: their chief charge is keeping people safe, not getting them to play or swim. They constantly monitor the children in their charge, which means they are moving around all the time. Movement should be random and vigilant; good supervisors are constantly aware of where children are and what they are doing.

Because most problems occur within the first five minutes of a play period, at least one supervisor should be stationed in the playground before the children arrive to ensure that everything there is safe. One person should be designated for this duty for each play period. All equipment and surfacing materials should be scrutinized to ensure that they are in good condition. On-the-spot supervisors should divert children from areas or activities that they aren't ready to use or that might be sources of conflict. The SAFE supervisory checklist in appendix A can help you make this preplay assessment quickly, thoroughly, and consistently.

Proper Positioning

Playground safety depends to a large extent on monitoring children from a variety of positions. Untrained or inadequate supervisors often stand in one place through-out a play period; competent supervisors move constantly throughout their areas of responsibility. Studies have demonstrated that safety problems increase when children can predict supervisors' movements, so good monitors move about unpredictably (Hudson, Olsen, Thompson, and Bruya 2010), weaving in and around playground equipment. If possible, changing elevation should be part of good practice too.

Scanning

Besides moving around, supervisors should actively scan the area they are mon-itoring, looking up and down, side to side, over and under. Competent scanning engages children in eye-to-eye, nonverbal contact to inhibit conflicts and possible injuries. When children know they are being watched, they are less likely to engage in risky behavior.

Focusing on Children, Not Peers

Interactions between a supervisor and other adults should be brief and supervi-sion related. It is impossible to adequately monitor children while conversing with a peer. If a peer's needs must be dealt with immediately, a supervisor should ask another person to take over her duties; she should not absent herself without a substitute. Adequate supervision is her moral and legal duty.

Equally, a supervisor's responsibility is toward all the children in her care. If one child needs special attention, the monitor should continue to scan the entire area. If she must divert her attention to a single child, then she should use her cell phone, whistle, hand signals, walkie-talkie, or a student messenger to request a replacement so she can leave her post.

Managing Behavior

All too often, supervisors witness inappropriate playground behavior (for example, bullying, teasing, misuse of equipment, quarrels over scarce materials). Programs should ensure that all supervisory staff have been trained in techniques for managing children's behavior and that everyone uses the same approaches. These range from unobtrusive ways of reminding children of the program's expectations—for example, eye contact, redirection, and compliments—to more active approaches, like setting clear, appropriate expectations, outlining rules, and reinforcing appropriate behavior. When these milder approaches prove inadequate, supervisors should correct children immediately, because they are likely to be endangering themselves or others by their behavior. Time-outs or removal to a quiet zone are appropriate.

Like adults, children are more likely to use an area safely and happily when they have been involved in designing it. Early childhood programs and schools can bring children into the design and building of their own playgrounds. They are likely to remember rules when they help write them themselves. They can also learn through modeling how to talk about safe and unsafe use of equipment so they can talk comfortably with their playmates when they witness hazardous behavior.

Setting expectations for playground behavior is important; the major outcome of establishing expectations, or rules, is a long-term commitment to safety. Expectations should be developed by all those who use the playground: the children, teachers, supervisors, and staff. Expectations should be limited to a small number in order for the children to learn and follow them (Thompson, Hudson, and Olsen, 2007).

Following is an example of playground expectations for children:

CHARACTER COUNTS ON THE PLAYGROUND

Caring: Treat others as you want to be treated.

Fairness: Take turns and play fair.

Respect: Be responsible for your actions.

Trustworthiness: Play by the rules and tell the truth.

Citizenship: Take care of the play area and treat it with respect.

And here is an example of playground expectations for playground supervisors:

POSITIVE PLAYGROUND SUPERVISION

Interact

- Get to know the children's names.
- Provide friendly rather than hostile supervision.
- Make positive contact with children who struggle to follow playground expectations.
- Interact three times more frequently with children when they are following the rules than when they are breaking them.

Circulate

- Cover all the areas where children play.
- Coordinate with other supervisors.
- Refocus children inclined to cling toward play.

Manage behavior

- Implement established playground expectations calmly.
- Keep verbal instructions short and simple.
- Keep consequences as mild as possible: verbal reminders of positive play behaviors; redirection; removal ("Follow me and be my helper").

Responding to Emergencies

Supervisors need to plan for emergencies (fig. 2.1.) Doing so should involve not only supervisors but also administrators, teachers, children, emergency medical technicians (EMTs) serving your program, and school or community nurses. The emergency plan should cover the following:

- alerting appropriate personnel
- managing other children
- coordinating communications among staff (for example, cell phones, walkie-talkies)
- designating first-aid providers among staff
- contacting EMTs and other emergency care providers

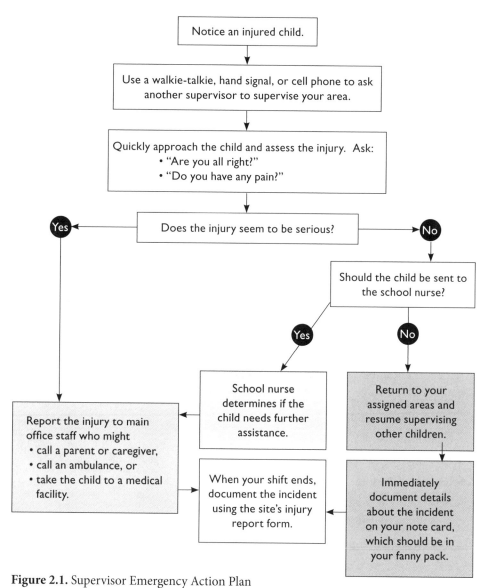

Figure 2.1. Supervisor Emergency Action Plan

Reprinted from *S.A.F.E. Play Areas: Creation, Maintenance, and Renovation* by D. Thompson,
S. Hudson, and H. Olsen (Champaign, IL: Human Kinetics, 2007).

Reporting Injuries

Injury report forms are critical to eliminating preventable accidents; they can help you pinpoint hazards and patterns of injuries. For example, are children being hurt by falling, bumping into equipment, or colliding with each other? The more exhaustively you document the causes of injuries, the more accurately you can determine how to prevent them in the future.

Injury report forms should include type of injury and description of how and where it occurred. (Sample injury report forms covering playground injuries can be found in appendix B.) Locating the site of an injury is often easier said than done; children frequently show up in the nurse's office or at the side of a playground supervisor to say that they have hurt themselves. The NPPS has found that in the absence of more detailed information, supervisors often fill out injury forms stating that children have hurt themselves on the "monkey bars" (Hudson, Olsen, and Thompson 2008b). This catchall phrase describes a variety of equipment that may not even be present and that doesn't help to determine the cause of the injury. Staff should be trained to know the names of each piece of equipment in the playground and to use them in filling out injury report forms so accurate pictures emerge of injury patterns. Develop your own injury report form, because it will serve the needs of your program, setting, staff, and children better than a standard one. For your injury report form to be as useful as possible, be sure that it includes the following information:

- location of injury
- cause of injury
- parts of body injured
- type of injury
- first-aid provided at facility
- first-aid provider
- people contacted about injury and time of contact
- agencies contacted
- follow-up plan for child's care
- corrective action needed to prevent similar injuries
- signatures of staff members and parents
  (US Department of Health and Human Services 2009)

Adequate Staffing Levels for Supervision

The number of supervisors needed on playgrounds should be planned in advance, taking into account the size of the area, the mandated levels of supervision, the number and ages of children, and the kinds of equipment available to them.

In the primary school environment, staff-to-student ratios as high as one supervisor to 150 children are not uncommon. In the child care environment, the NAEYC, the American Public Health Association (APHA), and the AAP have indicated that the staff-to-child ratio affects the quality of care the child care provider can give to each child. The ratio of staff to children will vary depending on age of the children, the type of program, the inclusion of children with special needs, the time of day, and the size of the play environment.

Practical implications, state regulations, and legal precedents all determine the appropriate ratios. To learn about your state's required staff-to-child ratio, contact your state's child care licensing department or department of education.

In child care and preschool environments, the staff need to discuss the difference between supervision and play facilitation. Often teachers are present on the playground, but they are engaged in the children's activities. If a teacher is outside and needs to be fully engaged in the children's activities, then another teacher must be supervising the children. For instance, let's say two classroom teachers take a group of twelve toddlers out into the play environment. One teacher takes four children to the sand-and-water table to make mud pies while the other teacher supervises the rest of the area. In this case, the teacher who is at the sand-and-water table is a play facilitator and would not be considered an appropriate supervisor even though there is a staff-to-child ratio of two to twelve. Since one teacher is fully engaged at the sand-and-water table, it is best to have an additional adult supervising the children. Then, two supervisors and one play facilitator would be present.

Discussion Questions

1. Select a school or child care playground and visit it when the site is in use. Note the ages of children on the site. Sketch the playground, including the location of equipment and the number of supervisors you see on the grounds. Draw the movement of supervisors around the playground, and see if you can characterize their locations in relation to the children on the ground.

2. Create a list of eight supervisory duties that you would include in writing a supervision policy for that playground.

Chapter 3

SAFE Age-Appropriate Design

Playground equipment should match the developmental skills and abilities of the children using it. This truism is far more complex than it may initially seem, for children not only develop at different rates, but their individual abilities also develop at varying rates—for instance, a child whose gross-motor skills are typical or even advanced for her age might still have depth perception more typical of a much younger child.

If children's development is typical, they are **challenged** by appropriate equipment—that is, their courage, their gross-motor skills, and their coordination are summoned to do things within their abilities, even though they may not yet be aware of those abilities. Because challenging play is not developmentally beyond their abilities, these children are probably not at risk—in real danger—because of the structures they are exploring or their own lack of experience. They *need* challenges to master; if equipment is undemanding, they are more likely to be drawn to play that represents not only challenges but also risks. These are two reasons why effective **supervision** is so intertwined with age-appropriate design in **SAFE** playgrounds: children need adults who are familiar with their development and abilities to ensure that their play is challenging, not risky.

Age-Appropriate Design

The good playground minimizes risks and creates developmentally appropriate challenges. Its challenges are appropriate to children of differing ages and abilities. In this chapter, we will describe age-appropriate design for children aged six months to twelve years.

ABC Elementary School decided to build a new outdoor playground for its students. The administrators asked for advice from trained playground consultants and then built three new areas for children in grades K–1, 2–3, and 4–6. They selected playground equipment that was developmentally appropriate for each of those age levels. The equipment was purchased from two companies. They installed appropriate **surfacing** from one company under and around elevated equipment. The surfacing and equipment complied with the **ASTM International** (formerly American Society for Testing and Materials, or ASTM) **standards** on two of the new play areas. To cut costs, the Parent-Teacher Association (PTA) asked an Eagle Scout to make a slide for the K–1 play area. The PTA also installed very inexpensive, slippery surfacing under the equipment in that play area.

Rita, a kindergartner, used the slide built by the Eagle Scout, and when she reached the bottom, she slipped off and fell, hitting her head on it. Rita became severely brain damaged, and her parents sued the school for more than $1 million. An investigation proved that the slide didn't meet ASTM International's standards: its anchors hadn't been installed at the appropriate depth, the surfacing surrounding it was not of the appropriate depth, nor was the slide properly installed. Agencies need to be careful to buy, install, and maintain equipment that complies with recognized standards and **guidelines**.

Creating Challenge

Challenge is the difficulty someone feels in completing a task successfully, the subjective feeling that the activity is arousing and demanding (Hudson and Thompson 1999). Challenges for children are intimately connected to their developmental readiness. For example, the challenge to children who are developmentally capable of climbing the stairs of a 6-foot (1.8 m.) slide may be similar to that of climbing a 10-foot (3 m.) slide. But the greater height creates a greater risk than the lower slide because young children may not be ready yet to descend the taller slide and may become stuck at the top. If they were to fall from the top of the higher slide, their risk of injury would be greater than from the top of the lower slide.

Figures 3.1a, 3.1b. Children are more likely to misuse playground equipment if it does not match their developmental stage.

The challenges posed by playground equipment should match, not exceed, children's developmental stage in order to be rousing and relatively safe. The reverse is also true: if children find equipment too easy to use because their abilities exceed its demands, they are more likely to misuse the equipment—for instance, decide to go down the slide backward or walk down it on their hands—and become injured (fig. 3.1).

Ideally, a playground offers high play value (challenge) and low risk. Your task, then, is to create stimulating play spaces that minimize the risk of injury to children without making their play too easy. To accomplish this, you will need to take their developmental stages into account. Unfortunately, this sometimes fails to happen. Too often the purchase of equipment is left to PTAs and Parent-Teacher Organizations (PTOs) that receive little guidance from the programs they serve, the vendors they buy from, or the organizations that have created guidelines and standards for playgrounds and playground equipment. The result is that playgrounds are sometimes not developmentally appropriate for children (Thompson, Hudson, and Olsen 2007).

Developmentally Appropriate Heights

No question about it: children love to climb, and they rapidly become adept at it. Especially among the youngest children, the problem is less one of climbing to a height than of getting down from it. The skills needed for climbing are not developmentally the same as those for sliding or climbing down. The result is that many two- to four-year-olds climb to the top of equipment designed for older children, only to stand rooted at the top. One recent study found that toddlers and preschoolers become frightened and sometimes freeze up when they reach the top of tall platforms; for example, in one case, "a child began crying and stamping his feet until a parent came and helped him down from the equipment" (Frost et al. 2004, 78). However, children can exhibit similar behavior on lower equipment too—it all depends on the child.

Children Aged Six to Twenty-Three Months

Children at six months are just beginning to become mobile, starting to turn over by themselves. This is why six to twenty-three months is an age category for playground equipment standards. Special considerations should be taken when designing playgrounds for this age category. These very young children have little understanding of cause and effect. For example, because they don't understand that hot surfaces can burn them, shade should be provided for the equipment they use.

Children in this age category are at the beginning of their physical, intellectual, emotional, and social development, and they need settings in which they can creep, crawl, walk, and fall safely. Cement or asphalt should not be used in areas where children are still learning to walk and are prone to fall. Pathway surfaces for six- to twenty-three-month-olds should be soft, such as rubber tiles or poured-in-place materials, and lead from building doors to play settings to facilitate children's ability to move on their own. These softer surfaces are safer and decrease the severity of injuries, but are also more expensive. They may, however, decrease the maintenance needed. When softer surfacing is used in a controlled environment, such as a child care facility, where vandalism and misuse are less likely to occur, the soft surfacing should last for many years and offset its original cost.

Preschoolers

Climbing is as necessary to young children as walking on horizontal surfaces; both activities are developmentally appropriate. But so, too, is fear of heights. When children begin to walk, their fear of heights increases (Bertenthal, Campos, and Barrett 1984). Walking is a better predictor of fear of heights than age among young children, for first learning to move around on two feet inevitably brings falls (Campos, Bertenthal, and Kermoian 1992; Gottlieb 1983, 1991). For children to overcome their fear of falling or their fear of heights, they "must be allowed to assume reasonable risks in order to develop cognitive and locomotor skills, yet be protected from extreme hazards" caused by their immaturity (Frost, Wortham, and Reifel 2011, 58). Because of this, the NPPS recommends play equipment for preschool children be limited to 6 feet (1.8 m.) or less.

Older Children

As children grow older and more physically adept, climbing isn't only about seeing what's above them or about reaching, say, the top of a slide; instead, they view it as an end in itself, a play experience. As one child put it, "'I'm going to outer space and driving'" (Frost et al. 2004, 75). What, then, might be the relationship between climbing and imagination in creating a play experience? Is height a significant enough factor in such experiences to offset increased risks of falling?

In our observations, the answer is no. Sliding down a 10-foot (3 m.) slide does not offer a significantly greater challenge than using an 8-foot (2.4 m.) slide. Climbing an 8-foot (2.4 m.) ladder is not more complex than climbing a 6-foot (1.8 m.) slide. A crow's nest elevated 12 feet (3.7 m.) above the ground or a 14-foot (4.3 m.) slide is no more likely to spark children's imagination than one that is lower. But in all these cases, a fall from higher equipment significantly increases children's risk of injury.

Tall equipment is definitely tempting to adults who plan and create playgrounds. Ask yourself, though, if tall structures would have looked as appealing when you were 3 or 4 feet (0.9 or 1.2 m.) tall. Too often, playground equipment is bought by adults who are excited by it. That's a poor criterion for selecting it; instead, look for equipment that is developmentally appropriate for the children who will be using it. Challenge them with complexity, not just with height.

In chapter 4, we will discuss the relationships between the height and velocity of falls, the potential for serious injury, and the mitigating effects of effective **fall surfaces**. For now, we wish only to challenge the widely held beliefs that tall play structures are inherently more exciting and no more dangerous than shorter ones for young children. Our recommendation is that equipment should be made more challenging, not merely higher.

The safety officer at a US military base in Asia contacted the NPPS several years ago because school administrators of a school on the base hoped to install a play structure 20 feet (6.1 m.) high on the school's playground. The faculty and the safety officer at the base opposed the idea, but the civil engineers working with the school assured its administrators that their calculations indicated that no serious injury would occur if children fell off the structure. After several e-mail exchanges, including the sharing of research documents attesting to the relationship between equipment height and injury and the doubling of probable injuries in equipment higher than 6 feet (1.8 m.), the school administrators chose not to build children the 20-foot (6.1 m.) thrill.

Figure 3.2. A playground for ages five to twelve.

Age-Appropriate Design

Children typically develop in predictable ways, although wide variance exists in their individual skill levels. Activities and equipment that are developmentally appropriate can be challenging but need not be very risky. Most of you know when children are ready to try balancing on a bicycle, go down a slide alone, or climb on a playground structure. Readiness doesn't eliminate challenge until children have thoroughly mastered a skill; even then, it may offer a familiar pleasure. By providing equipment for developmentally appropriate play, you minimize the risk that children may injure themselves. This is why playgrounds need to offer equipment that is challenging to a range of ages and abilities. The following table lists a variety of playground equipment and denotes the appropriate ages for each.

Table 3.1. Play Equipment for Different Age Groups

Equipment	*	Preschool Ages				School Age						
	6–23 mo.	2	3	4	5	6	7	8	9	10	11	12
CONSTRUCTIVE												
Sand Diggers			x	x	x	x						
Sand Play Tables	x	x	x	x	x	x	x					x
SOCIAL												
Playhouse	x	x	x	x	x							x
Mazes		x	x	x	x							
Storefronts		x	x	x	x							
Play Panels	x	x	x	x	x	x						x
SLIDES												
Double Slides		x	x	x	x	x						
48' Spiral		x	x	x	x	x						
64' Slides			x	x	x	x	x	x	x	x		
Tunnel					x	x	x	x	x	x		
Fire Poles								x	x	x	x	x
CLIMBERS												
Arch Climber							x	x	x	x	x	x
Curly Climber								x	x	x	x	x
Hoop Climber								x	x	x	x	
Chain Net					x	x	x	x				
UPPER BODY STRENGTH												
Parallel Bars					x	x	x	x	x	x	x	x
Horizontal Ladder					x	x	x	x	x	x	x	x
Challenge/S Horizontal Ladder								x	x	x	x	x
Ring Ladders								x	x	x	x	x

*Infant/Toddler Ages

Table 3.1. Play Equipment for Different Age Groups, cont.

Equipment	*	Preschool Ages				School Age						
	6–23 mo.	2	3	4	5	6	7	8	9	10	11	12
BALANCE												
Balance Beam					x	x	x	x	x	x	x	x
Curved Beam					x	x	x	x	x	x	x	x
Moving Beam							x	x	x	x	x	x
MOVING												
Spring Rockers			x	x	x							
Infant Enclosed Swing	x	x	x	x	x							
Belt Swing					x	x	x	x	x	x		
Tire Swing				x	x	x	x	x	x	x		
Seesaw		x	x	x	x	x	x	x	x	x		
Multi-seesaw			x	x	x	x	x	x	x	x	x	x
Log Roll							x	x	x	x	x	x

*Infant/Toddler Ages

Areas for Children Six Months to Twenty-Three Months

In community parks, equipment for very young children (aged six to twenty-three months), young children (ages two to five years), and older children (aged five to twelve years) should be separate. These should be divided into several spaces based on the developmental abilities of the children. Separate spaces should be created for those who do not walk yet (children up to twelve months) and those who are starting to walk (up to twenty-three months). Children who do not walk yet are often uninvolved in the action around them and instead participate as onlookers. Areas designed for them should reflect this behavior and offer activities these children can do by themselves.

Aspect of Playground	Appropriate for 6–23 Months
Surfacing	Soft, smooth, even surfacing should be provided for pathways.
Playground equipment	Based on ASTM F2373 standards and specifically designed for children aged 6 to 23 months.
Spaces	Room for playing with manipulative objects like cars, trucks, and balls on their own and away from playground equipment.
Footage	At least 75 square feet (22.9 sq. m.) for each child playing outside at the same time (NAEYC 2014).
Shade	One-third of play area should be shaded to protect very young children (NAEYC 2014).

Areas for Children Aged Two to Three Years

The NPPS recommends that children aged two to five years be further divided into groups of two to three and four to five years old. Too often, particularly in community parks, play equipment is available only for two- to five- and five- to twelve-year-olds. The equipment for younger children is often more limited in variety, causing these children to be drawn to the larger, more varied, and more complex equipment intended for older children. The result is that younger children may climb onto developmentally inappropriate equipment and become injured or get run over by larger children.

Playground equipment for children aged two to three years should provide stability and offer places for children to grasp on to while exploring the area and equipment. Playground equipment for children in this age range must meet the ASTM International F1487 standard, which addresses safety and performance standards for playground equipment intended for public use. Accommodations should also be made for children with special needs so they can get into and out of the area and use its equipment. If space is limited, areas for children two to three years old can be combined with those for children four to five years old.

Aspect of Playground	Appropriate for 2–3 Years
Surfacing	Soft, smooth, even surfacing should be provided for pathways.
Playground equipment	Based on ASTM 1487 standard and the *CPSC Public Handbook*. Two- and 3-year-olds are still egocentric and need objects of their own to play with. Structures should be distanced from each other to avoid children falling on each other. Provide places for stability for new walkers to keep themselves balanced. Steps, slides, and balance beams 1 foot (0.3 m.) wide are good choices.
Spaces	Room for game areas, bird feeders, and short climbing structures are appropriate. Spaces for playing games with objects like balls should be distant from playground equipment.
Footage	At least 75 square feet (22.9 sq. m.) for each child playing outside at the same time (NAEYC 2014).
Fall height	Defined by the CPSC as the height from the highest designated surface of a play structure to the **fall surface**). No more than 6 feet (1.8 m.).

Areas for Children Aged Four to Five Years

Children in this age range are more adept at large movements than at fine-motor skills. They can manipulate objects and descend ladders by alternating their feet. They may need places to jump and hop. If space is limited, areas for children aged four to five years can be combined with those for children aged two to three years.

Aspect of Playground	Appropriate for 4–5 Years
Surfacing	Paths can curve, change in pitch, and offer smooth and rough areas. A variety of materials should be used to minimize the hazard of tripping.
Playground equipment	Based on ASTM 1487 standard and the *CPSC Public Handbook*. Includes 1-foot- (.3 m.) wide balance beams, short ladders, sandboxes, a house that can become a fire station or a home, swings, trikes, and climbing structures. Tables for game playing, painting, or reading. Nearby storage for equipment.
Spaces	Paths for trikes; separate areas for table-based play and climbing structures.
Footage	At least 75 square feet (22.9 sq. m.) for each child playing outside at the same time (NAEYC 2005).

Areas for Children Aged Five to Twelve Years

Although the ASTM International F1487 standard specifies the entire age range five to twelve, equipment is available that is better suited to children within narrower age ranges; we suggest that you focus separately on grades K–1, 2–3, and 4–6.

Take, for example, track rides: although these systems are marketed as suited to a wide range of young children, children younger than eight years old find them very difficult to use independently. This is because these younger children lack the balance, arm strength, and grip necessary to remain safe while the ride traverses the rail. Not surprisingly, the injury rate for track rides in elementary schools is highest among children in the five-to-six-years-old category.

Aspect of Playground	Appropriate for 5–12 Years
Surfacing	Paths can curve, change in pitch, and offer smooth and rough areas.
Playground equipment	Stand-alone climbing structures, climbing structures that encourage upper body development, climbing walls, balance beams, swings, open grassy areas, hard surface areas for games.
Spaces	Paths for bikes; separate areas for table-based play, climbing structures, and open space.
Footage	At least 75 square feet (22.9 sq. m.) for each child playing outside at the same time (NAEYC).

Sunnyside Elementary School stands next to the Hudson Community Park, so it seemed only logical that the school and town would share playground equipment. Over the years, the school and the local parks and recreation department worked out an informal agreement: PTA paid for equipment and updates of the playground, and P&R provided maintenance. The school had exclusive rights to the playground from 7:30 a.m. to 3:00 p,m,; the rest of the time, anyone could use it. Because school-age children were the chief users, the PTA bought playground equipment designed for five- to twelve-year-olds. Then the school began a pre-K program before raising funds for or creating developmentally appropriate play equipment for preschool children.

On an October day, four-year-old Quisha ran outside and climbed atop an 8-foot (2.4 m.) high geodesic dome in the center of the playground. She lost her grip and fell through the structure to the ground, which was covered in 2 inches (5.1 cm.) of wood chips. The chips failed to insulate the impact of Quisha's fall, and the growth plates in both her legs broke.

Faced with mounting medical bills and possible lifelong complications from their daughter's injury, Quisha's parents sued the school district and the city for damages. The school and P&R could have foreseen and prevented possible injury to Quisha, but they failed to provide adequate fall surfacing and equipment suitable to the age and developmental stage of a child using it, and there was a lack of supervision. The suit was settled out of court.

Children with Disabilities

The needs of children who develop atypically because of physical, emotional, social, or intellectual disabilities must be taken into account in the design and maintenance of SAFE playgrounds. Since the 1990 passage of the federal Americans with Disabilities Act, **universal design** has provided children with disabilities access to the same play areas as typically developing children. In most cases, children with disabilities are also able to use the same equipment as other children. Active, thoughtful supervision (see chapter 2) is particularly important for children with learning disabilities; they are unlikely to possess the same coordination or ability to assess possible risks as typically developing children of their age. Designing playgrounds to accommodate children at a wide variety of developmental stages, typical and atypical, is challenging. It must start with recognizing what children are typically capable of at different stages and ages and finding the equipment that suits them. It is easier to change equipment than to change children. Newly built or retrofitted playgrounds must now use universal design to ensure they can be enjoyed by children of differing abilities. Disabilities that must be factored into design include the following:

- cognitive delay
- hearing impairment
- speed or language impairment
- visual impairment
- serious emotional disturbance
- orthopedic impairment
- autism
- traumatic brain injury
- specific learning disabilities
  (Brault 2012)

With the exception of getting into and out of playgrounds, most children with disabilities can be accommodated with thoughtful and attentive adult supervision. For example, children with developmental delays may need to use equipment designed for younger children; children with autism may need to be directed to equipment that is appropriate to their level of motor control or strength; children with cochlear transplants should not use plastic slides, whose friction may disrupt and destroy these children's transplants. Playground equipment itself can be modified to accommodate some disabilities: for example, some manufacturers now provide Braille inscriptions on their structures for children with impaired vision.

Good playgrounds not only make their delights accessible, but they also minimize risk by providing equipment and surfaces that are firm, stable, and slip
resistant. (ADA guidelines for playgrounds cover children ages two to twelve; see
appendix C for ADA guideline checklist.)

Use National Guidelines and Standards

A lot of thought, passion, inquiry, cooperation, and experience have gone into
devising playground safety standards and guidelines over the past forty-odd years.
Your first stop in planning or rethinking playgrounds should be to familiarize yourself with these standards and guidelines, including ones issued by the US Department of Justice (DOJ) under the 1990 ADA. States, school districts, Parks and
Recreation departments, local child care agencies, and other organizations have
either adopted, adapted, or recommend those described here. Find out what, if any,
guidelines and standards are applicable to your play area.

Guidelines and standards for playground safety are a mixture of voluntary and
statutory, reflecting the many attempts that have been made to regulate playground
supervision, surfaces, and equipment. The two most influential organizations to
have developed standards, guidelines, and regulations for minimizing playground
risks are the Consumer Product Safety Commission and ASTM International. The
CPSC guidelines and ASTM International standards address several age groups:
six to twenty-three months, two to five years, and five to twelve years (CPSC 2010,
ASTM International F1487 2011, ASTM International F2373 2011,).

Here are brief descriptions of the agencies and organizations that have issued
recognized guidelines or standards that address playground safety.

US Consumer Product Safety Commission

The CPSC was created in 1972 with passage of the federal Consumer Product Safety
Act. The commission is charged with

1. protecting the public against unreasonable risk of injury and death from consumer products,
2. assisting the public in evaluating the comparative safety of products,
3. developing uniform safety standards for consumer products, and
4. promoting research and investigation into the causes of product-related
   deaths, illnesses, and injuries (Kitzes 2001).

The CPSC introduced its first set of guidelines for playgrounds in 1981, in *Handbook for Public Playground Safety*. A second handbook, this one for home playgrounds, was issued in 2005. The most recent update to its guidelines can be found in the CPSC's 2010 *Public Playground Safety Handbook*.

It is important to keep the CPSC's guidelines in mind even after playground equipment has been installed, because the agency issues recalls of faulty playground equipment. To see the complete CPSC 2010 handbook, visit www.cpsc.gov /PageFiles/122149/325.pdf.

ASTM International

This venerable engineering organization (founded in 1898) has developed voluntary standards for everything from bridge-steel strength to clean water, football helmets, and playground fall surfaces and equipment. In the 1970s, ASTM International (then known as American Society for Testing and Materials), at the urging of members who were playground equipment manufacturers, approached the CPSC suggesting that ASTM International develop technical specifications for playground equipment. The CPSC agreed, and ASTM International issued its first standards in 1988. Since then, it has developed a wide range of playground standards, including standards for the following:

- surfacing
- home playground equipment
- climbing walls
- amusement rides
- public-use playground equipment
- fencing
- soft, contained play equipment used in restaurant play areas
- infant swings
- wood fiber
- play equipment for children aged six to twenty-three months
- poured-in-place surfacing
- aquatic playgrounds
- foam playground equipment

ASTM International's committee on public-use playground equipment is one of its largest, with over 170 members.

Americans with Disabilities Act (ADA)

A somewhat different set of developmentally appropriate guidelines has evolved through the US DOJ since passage of the ADA in 1990. The ADA mandates that public places be accessible to people with disabilities. These spaces include parks, playgrounds, schools, and publicly funded child care facilities. In 2010, ADA regulations were updated to provide access to playgrounds and play equipment to children with disabilities from two to twelve years of age. Regulations now cover ground and elevated play structures; accessible routes; transfer systems; ground surfaces; and soft, contained play structures (US Department of Justice 2010; Hudson et al. 2009). These and subsequent publications focus on three compliance criteria under the ADA:

- ability to move from the edge of the playground to the equipment
- opportunity to play with other children
- ability to move from equipment to the edge of the playground and into a parking lot or building

Other Organizations Advocating for Playground Safety

Besides the guidelines and standards of the CPSC, ASTM International, and the ADA, other organizations promote playground safety. The Infant/Toddler Environment Rating Scale (ITERS) and Early Childhood Environment Rating Scale (ECERS) offer rating scales you can use to assess your playground's safety.

Consult the resource list on page 137 for links to the following groups that advocate for playground safety:

American Academy of Pediatrics, American Public Health Association, and National Resource Center for Health and Safety in Child Care and Early Education

Working together, these organizations have issued three editions of their standards and guidelines, *Caring for Our Children: National Health and Safety Performance Standards: Guidelines for Early Care and Education Programs* (third edition, 2011). These include standards for playground size, location, playground and play area equipment, surfacing, inspection, and outdoor play equipment. Many state agencies are required to comply with these standards and guidelines. The book also contains child injury report forms, a safety report card, and a follow-up playground safety report card adapted from NPPS materials.

Early Childhood Environmental Rating Scale (ECERS-R)

Published by Teacher College Press in 2005, this revised edition focuses on safety in child care settings for children from two and a half through five years of age. It includes information on assessing indoor spaces, room arrangements for play, sand and water play, free play, spaces for gross-motor play, gross-motor equipment, supervision of gross-motor skills, general supervision of children, safety practices, provisions for children with disabilities, and other aspects of care (Harms, Clifford, and Cryer 2005).

Infant/Toddler Environmental Rating Scale Revised Edition (ITERS-R)

Published by Teachers College Press in 2006, the revised edition of the ITERS highlights safety in child care settings for children from birth to thirty months old. It includes information on assessing indoor spaces, safety practices, active physical play, sand and water play, supervision of play and learning, free-play activities, provisions for children with disabilities, and other aspects of early care (Harms, Cryer, and Clifford 2006).

National Association for the Education of Young Children (NAEYC)

NAEYC is the largest organization in the United States offering guidance to child care centers, facilities, and providers of family child care. Presentations about playground safety have been included in its national conventions for more than twenty years. The organization's national guidelines for supervision ratios and playground inspections are well known and often used by local and state agencies. NAEYC has also issued recommendations on shading for outdoor playgrounds.

National Health and Safety Performance Standards

The American Public Health Association and the American Academy of Pediatrics jointly published *Caring for Our Children: National Health and Safety Performance Standards; Guidelines for Out-of-Home Child Care Programs* in 1992, which includes information on playground safety. Subsequent editions have addressed what has been learned through increased research into health and safety in early care and education programs.

National Program for Playground Safety (NPPS)

The NPPS raises awareness of playground safety and works to prevent playground injuries through its workshops, publications, and online certification courses. The organization trains and certifies early childhood playground inspectors, elementary school playground inspectors, supervisors of child care center and school playgrounds, and maintenance staff of child care, school, and park playgrounds.

State of Virginia

The most comprehensive standards for playgrounds issued by a state are those of Virginia. *From Playgrounds to Play/Learning Environments* (DeMary and Ramnarain 2003) covers development of age-appropriate learning environments, curriculum, planning, implementation, and CPSC's and ASTM International's guidelines and standards.

US Department of Defense

The DOD developed Unified Facilities Criteria for designing child development centers at air force, navy, and marine installations (US Department of Defense 2002). Criteria cover supervision, age-appropriate areas for infants, pre-toddlers, and toddlers (not for older children), CPSC guidelines, ASTM International standards, children with special needs, surfacing, fencing, shade, and **use zones**.

US Department of Health and Human Services, Administration for Children and Families, Administration on Children, Youth and Families, and Office of Head Start

These four organizations combined to write *Head Start Design Guide: A Guide for Building a Head Start Facility* (National Head Start Training, 2005), which offers suggestions and guidelines for planning and designing Head Start centers. It addresses the amount of space recommended for physical environments, different kinds of play activities, playground surfacing, fencing, toxic and nontoxic plant materials, health and safety of facilities, and a playground safety inspection guide.

Kokomo Elementary School had recently expanded its facility to include a preschool classroom. The new room was carefully and thoughtfully designed to serve the needs of three- to five-year-olds. But the school grounds were a different story. The playground area, developed for children ages five to twelve, remained unaltered. No changes were made to accommodate the new, younger students at the school. Since there was no equipment provided specifically for the children in their care, the early childhood teachers decided to allow them to play on the existing playground equipment.

One day four-year-old Hannah was playing on the 7-foot- (2.1 m.) high horizontal ladder. Another student had lifted her to reach the rungs and was attempting to hold on to Hannah as she moved across them. Despite that student's efforts, Hannah fell to the ground and broke her arm.

The preschool teachers had not put any restrictions on the use of equipment. They assumed that their children could play on anything as long as they were playing at a different time than the older children. They learned their lesson the hard way from Hannah's injury: the school was sued by Hannah's family, and the suit was settled out of court.

Compliance with Guidelines and Standards

Guidelines and standards vary widely. The ADA's provisions are mandatory nationwide, while the guidelines and standards issued by the CPSC, ASTM International, and other organizations committed to playground safety have been adopted by a number of states, cities, state and local boards of education, and school systems. Some states have developed their own (see appendix D). California demands compliance with both CPSC and ASTM International. The US DOD has created its own standards, which adhere to CPSC guidelines and ASTM International standards.

Although the guidelines and standards we have reviewed here may lack statutory power in your own area, they are important to incorporate into the design and maintenance of SAFE playgrounds. Should you ignore them, your program may be open to a liability suit when a child becomes injured.

Talking Points on Playground Safety from the CPSC's 2009 Data

Facts culled from the CPSC's 2009 data on playground injuries can help you demonstrate the importance of your own safety program. Here are some persuasive talking points based on data from 2001–2008:

- Swings, slides, climbers, and horizontal ladders were involved in 57 percent of playground injuries.
- Sites of playground injuries included child care (39 percent), home (28 percent), restaurants (15 percent), parks (8 percent), and schools (4 percent).
- Equipment most often cited in injuries was swings or swing sets (22 percent), slides or sliding boards (17 percent), climbers (9 percent), and monkey bars (9 percent).
- Most common injuries were contusions or abrasions (56 percent) and fractures (33 percent).
- Percent of injuries by age were 0–4 years (32 percent) and 5–9 years (21 percent).
- Percent of injuries by sex were male (48 percent) and female (45 percent).
  (O'Brien 2009)

Using Guidelines and Standards to Reduce Playground Injuries

In 2003, the Iowa legislature granted the NPPS money to study surfacing and safe playground training for child care centers, elementary schools, and state parks. In a follow-up playground workshop, participants learned how to identify the most common playground hazards using CPSC, ASTM International, ADA, and other organizations' playground guidelines and standards. They reviewed best practices in supervising, planning, developmentally appropriate design, fall surfacing, and other topics.

The results of this training were significant: the safety training alone helped to reduce injuries by 50 percent from previous reported injury data. Combined with rubber safe-surfacing materials, the injury rate dropped by 76 percent from previous reported injury data (Olsen, Hudson, and Thompson 2003). The Iowa Safe Surfacing Initiative proves that applying existing guidelines and standards, offering appropriate training, and installing and maintaining good surfacing significantly reduces injuries. (SAFE surfacing is the topic of our next chapter.)

Vendors and Age-Appropriate Equipment

Finally, it is important to emphasize here that you must be your own advocate for the age appropriateness of playground equipment when you are dealing with vendors and distributors. You do not need to create or modify your playground simply because of a vendor's recommendations. You are the expert on supervising children; you know what is age appropriate for them. You have researched the equipment and surfaces that are as safe as possible for the children you serve, and you alone know what your resources are for maintaining equipment and grounds. As long as your choices comply with recognized guidelines and standards, vendors should modify their recommendations to suit you, not vice versa. Ask them to explain and justify their recommendations, and if you want only part of what they recommend, buy only that. If you want two slides rather than three, request them. If you prefer one vendor or distributor's climbing towers and another's swings, buy them separately. You're the client. Understand, however, that you cannot attach company A's equipment to company B's equipment (see chapter 5 for more on this topic).

To make sure that you get what you need to make children's outdoor play SAFE, our next chapter discusses in great detail what we mean by SAFE fall surfaces.

Discussion Questions

1. Visit a local child care center or early childhood program and observe how outdoor play space has been divided for different ages of children. Does equipment and surfacing differ by area? How?
2. Visit a local P&R playground to see if you can identify equipment, pathways, and play spaces that are ADA compliant.

Chapter 4

SAFE Fall Surfaces

In chapter 3, we discussed the importance of age- and developmentally appropriate play equipment for children. In this chapter, we will extend that discussion by looking at the need for appropriate shock-absorbing surfaces under and around play equipment. You will learn what is currently known about the mitigating effects of **fall surfaces** when children tumble from heights, how to choose effective fall surfacing, and how to maintain it.

Falls are the number one cause of children's unintentional injuries, and 79 percent of playground injuries involve falls onto unsafe surfaces, according to the **CPSC** (National Electronic Injury Surveillance System 2009). Installing appropriate fall surfaces under and surrounding playground equipment is the third of the four linchpins of **SAFE** playgrounds. We will tell you what is now known about the connections between height of equipment and speed of falls and the fall surfaces that can lessen the impact of falls. We will describe the surfaces that ensure that falls are as friendly as possible.

Fall Heights and Fall Surfacing

The CPSC's **guidelines** for **fall heights** vary with equipment, children's ages, and landing surfaces. If this is starting to sound like a three-dimensional chess game in its intricacy, you are right—the factors that go into insulating children's falls are many and complex. The chief ones, however, are equipment height and the surfaces below that equipment. Simply put, the higher children go on equipment, the harder they can fall; if the surfaces onto which they fall fail to adequately absorb the impact, children will be injured.

Five-year-old Andrew was looking forward to his first day of kindergarten. However, the weekend before starting school, his family took him to the park to enjoy some unstructured play. At the park, he ran to the old monkey bars that had stood in the park for decades. As he climbed up the 9-foot (2.7 m.) structure, he lost his grip and fell down through the bars. (The structure's interlocking bars were one reason that the CPSC had alerted consumers in the 1980s about the dangers of this type of equipment.) Hitting the bars didn't produce Andrew's major injury, although it did contribute to the more than two hundred bruises covering his body. Rather, it was the bolt sticking up from the ground, unprotected by adequate surfacing, that did the major damage. Andrew landed on the bolt and the hard surface beneath the play structure, severely damaging his jaw. Luckily, he survived this trip to the playground, and eighteen surgeries later, he is a handsome young man and a national playground safety advocate.

In developing **standards** and guidelines for safe playgrounds, the CPSC and **ASTM International** now measure two elements: acceleration from fall height and ability of surfaces to absorb the impact (the technical term for this is ***impact attenuation***) of children's falls. Researchers look at whether peak acceleration during impact exceeds the threshold of 200 times the acceleration (known as *200 g*; *G* is the technical term for ***gravity force***). A second value measures **deceleration** from a fall as well as the length of time it takes for deceleration to occur (that is, for the impact of a fall to be absorbed by the surface onto which someone falls). This is called the ***head injury criterion*** (**HIC**). Fall surfaces that yield peak deceleration below 200 g and HIC below 1,000 are unlikely to produce life-threatening head injuries (CPSC 2010, 8). (Appendix E describes fall heights for a variety of playground equipment.)

Table 4.1 demonstrates the relationship between fall height and acceleration for equipment ranging in height from 3 to 12 feet (0.9 to 3.7 m.). It is clear that the impact from a 12-foot (3.7 m.) fall is greater than that from an 8-foot (2.4 m.) fall.

Table 4.1. Height and Acceleration in Falls

Fall height of equipment	Distance traveled per second	Miles per hour
3 feet (0.9 m.)	13.8 feet (4.2 m.) per second	9.4 mph (15.1 kmh)
4 feet (1.22 m.)	16.1 feet (4.9 m.) per second	11.0 mph (17.7 kmh)
6 feet (1.83 m.)	19.7 feet (6.0 m.) per second	13.5 mph (21.7 kmh)
8 feet (2.44 m.)	22.6 feet (6.9 m.) per second	15.4 mph (24.8 kmh)
10 feet (3.05 m.)	25.3 feet (7.7.m.) per second	17.2 mph (27.7 kmh)
12 feet (3.7 m.)	27.7 feet (8.4 m.) per second	18.8 mph (30.3 kmh)

The formula for determining acceleration from height is:

Final velocity = v initial velocity + 2 (acceleration)(distance)

Effective Fall Surfaces

Suppose you buy, build, or adapt playground equipment whose fall heights are well within the CPSC's guidelines for your playground. Important as this is, it is not enough to ensure that falls from elevated equipment will not result in injuries, because the surfaces under and around play structures must be able to absorb the impact from children's falls without injuring them. Surfaces need to protect children's heads from impact at speeds that can reach 15-plus mph (24.1-plus kmh).

Effective fall surfaces help absorb the force of impacts and therefore shorten the peak deceleration of children's heads when they hit a surface. ASTM International recently devised testing protocol F1292 to assess the ability of surfaces under and around playground equipment to decelerate impact. Results demonstrated that playground surfaces differ widely in their ability to absorb the impact of falls, so choosing appropriate surfacing materials to use under and around equipment should be your first priority (fig. 4.1). Recommended materials for playground fall surfaces may be loose or unitary; what they have in common is their ability to absorb impact far more effectively than the hard-packed earth or asphalt that characterized playground surfaces of the past. Your second decision should be to match the selected surfacing materials to the height of playground equipment. Third, you should select the appropriate depth of material for the height of equipment. Fourth, you must match the fall surface to each **use zone**.

Figure 4.1. The SAFE Surfacing Decision Model

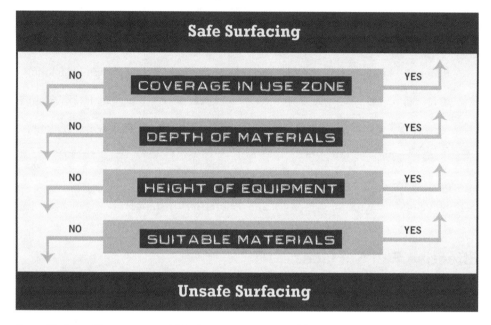

From Hudson, Thompson, and Mack 1999, 4. Reprinted by permission.

Loose Fill

Loose fill is the most popular material used in playgrounds. Loose fill consists of unbonded cushioning material. Its fall-absorbing ability depends on the air trapped between and within the loose fill. Because it can shift, it should never be installed over hard surfaces like asphalt, concrete, or packed earth. To remain effective, loose fill needs to be confined within barriers or an excavated area, and drainage must be effective so the fill retains loftiness and doesn't migrate.

In 2004, the NPPS found that 87 percent of surveyed playgrounds used loose fill for surfacing under and around playground equipment: 32 percent used wood chips, 23 percent used sand, 20 percent used wood fiber, and another 20 percent used pea gravel. Less than 2 percent used shredded rubber (Hudson, Olsen, and Thompson 2004).

What Kind of Loose Fill?

Each kind of loose fill offers advantages and disadvantages. In most of them, other materials can easily become mixed in (for example, dirt, broken glass, animal droppings); they can also become home to insects and other animals. Heavy metals are common in woody loose fill, unless it is obtained from manufacturers who certify its freedom from heavy metals. This is also true of shredded tires. Because loose fill can compact or scatter, it needs to be deeper than **unitary surfacing.**

Organic Materials

Organic loose-fill materials include wood chips, bark mulch, and engineered wood fibers; these are cut to ensure the fibers are uniform. Such materials eventually compact and decompose and must be regularly replaced. When wet, they can rot. If weeds and other plants appear on their surface, they are probably already decomposing (see fig. 4.2).

Figure 4.2. When weeds begin growing through the surface of loose fill, like at the base of this slide, it means the organic loose fill is decomposing and needs to be replaced.

Loose organic fill should be purchased from suppliers who specialize in playground surfacing and can demonstrate that their fill meets ASTM International F1292 standard and is made for use under and around playground equipment. Why? We have received reports that loose organic fill from community chipping operations can imperil children.

Some parks and recreation departments, city parks, and school districts use chippers to turn fallen branches, recycled Christmas trees, and other woody matter into chips. Heavy metals from fertilizers, insecticides, and Christmas-tree flocking compounds, nails, and other metals may find their way into such wood chips. When these materials are spread as loose fill, children become exposed to all of these chemicals and contaminants. Wood chips also emerge from chippers in different lengths, some of which are long, sharp, or bulky.

In regions where high winds are common, wood fill can dry up and blow away, while in very damp areas, wood fill may become a luxurious substrate for molds. Wood chips can also become weapons, intentionally or accidentally. For example, in a legal case one of us consulted on, a sizable chip thrown by one child at another during recess hit and blinded the second child in one eye.

Inorganic Materials

Most inorganic loose fills, including sand, pea gravel, and gravel, have recently declined in popularity. Because of their mass, they easily compact and must be occasionally loosened and aerated. If this isn't done, they can turn to hardpan (fig. 4.3). In extremely cold climates, sand can freeze into a rigid surface. If it is saturated with water, it can become hard and inflexible, the opposite of what you want in a cushioning fall surface. Sand also blows about and can be easily tracked back indoors, where it abrades rugs and floors. Gravel is a poor choice for children younger than five years of age because they are often inclined to put it into their ears, noses, and mouths.

Unitary Surfaces

These are fall-surfacing materials whose particles are bonded together. Rubber tiles or mats, poured urethane, and rubber compositions are the most common ones.

Unitary surfaces are more expensive because they must be installed by their manufacturer or expert contractors. Our 2004 NPPS study found that only 13 percent of surveyed playgrounds used unitary surfaces; 35 percent of these were rubber mats or tiles, and the rest were synthetic, poured-in-place products (Hudson, Olsen, and Thompson 2004). Any of these products is acceptable if it meets ASTM International F1292 guidelines.

Unitary surfaces are commonly low maintenance: they don't need to be contained, for they don't shift and degrade easily. They may, however, develop holes or cracks, so extra material for repairs should be purchased when the surfaces are installed. Unitary surfaces may be poor choices for playgrounds in extreme climates: where it is very cold, for example, permafrost can cause unitary fill to buckle; in extreme heat,

Figure 4.3. Hard-packed surfaces or grass under equipment don't offer enough protection from falls. Children are more likely to sustain a serious injury if they leap or fall from this swing set than if the surface beneath were loose fill or unitary surfacing.

unitary surfaces can become too hot for children to play on; and in areas that have an abundance of fog or moisture, these surfaces may become slippery.

The point is that there is no one best surface material. Rather, the chosen material should pass the SAC test—*standard* (whether it meets ASTM International F1292), *ages* (appropriate for the ages of the children using the playground), and *climate* (its ability to stand up to the weather in the area).

You can and probably should vary the kind of fill needed around and under playground equipment. For example, a unitary surface may be appropriate under a stand-alone piece of equipment, while loose fill may be a better choice for covering large areas, such as under swings. Do not mix surfacing materials—for example, 6 inches (15.2 cm.) of sand and 6 inches (15.2 cm.) of wood chips. Doing so cancels out the absorptive capacity of both materials.

How Does Height of Equipment Affect the Selection of Surfacing Materials?

The height of equipment limits your choice of appropriate surfacing materials for use under and around elevated equipment. Some surfaces, such as pea gravel, provide sufficient shock absorbency only for falls from relatively low heights, such as 6 feet (1.8 m.). No surfacing materials have been tested for equipment higher than 12 feet (3.7 m.), so no one can guarantee that any form of fill will absorb the shock of falls from that height. The following charts provide you with height restrictions for loose-fill and unitary surfacing materials.

Table 4.2. Adequate Loose-Fill Depths

Type of Fill	Fill Depth	Fall Height Protection
Shredded/recycled rubber	6 inches (15.2 cm.)	10 feet (3.1 m.)*
Wood chips	9 inches (23 cm.)	10 feet (3.1 m.)**
Sand	9 inches (23 cm.)	4 feet (1.2 m.)
Pea gravel	9 inches (23 cm.)	4 feet (1.2 m.)
Pea gravel	12 inches (30.5 cm.)	6 feet (1.8 m.)***

*Loose shredded/recycled rubber fill does not compress the same as other loose fill; it can shift more, so its depth must be continuously maintained for constant level.
**The NPPS and CPSC recommend 12 inches (30.5 cm) of wood chips be used because chips decompose with use.
***With heights of equipment greater than 6 feet (1.8 m.), pea gravel cannot safely absorb impact from falls, no matter how deep it is.
Source: *Public Playground Safety Handbook* 2010, 11

Table 4.3. Adequate Unitary-Fill Depths

Unitary Fill Depth	Fall Height Protection
2 inches (5 cm.)	5 feet (1.5 m.)
3 inches (7.5 cm.)	6–8 feet (1.8–2.4 m.)

Determining Slide Use Zones

The use zone at the exit end of the slide shall be the vertical distance of the slide based on the calculation that the exit region shall not be less than 6 feet (1.8 m.) but not more than 8 feet (2.4 m.). Thus,

- a slide the height of 6 feet (1.8 m.) would have a use zone exit of 6 feet (1.8 m.);
- a slide the height of 8 feet (2.4 m.) would have a use zone exit of 8 feet (2.4 m.); and
- a slide over the height of 8 feet (2.4 m.) would have an exit region of 8 feet (2.4 m.).

The use zone at the exit end of the slide should never overlap with the use zone of any other equipment. However, two or more slide use zones may overlap if their sliding paths are parallel.

What Areas Should Surfacing Materials Cover?

The safety zones under and around playground equipment that need appropriate playground surfacing materials are known as **use zones**.

The CPSC outlines requirements for use zones in its 2010 *Public Playground Safety Handbook*. In most cases, use zones extend 6 feet (1.8 m.) around stationary equipment. Swings and slides require extended use zones because children move on and off this equipment differently than they do other play structures. (Appendix F provides the use zones specified by the CPSC.) The CPSC's guidelines state that hard surfacing materials, such as asphalt or concrete, are unsuitable for use under and around playground equipment of any height unless they are required as a base for a shock-absorbing unitary material such as a rubber mat (CPSC 2010, 9). The guidelines do not recommend soil, hard-packed dirt, grass, or turf because they lack the absorptive quality of other kinds of surfaces (CPSC 2010).

Other Considerations Influencing Your Choice of SAFE Surfacing

While the type of materials, height of equipment, depth of surfacing materials, and use zones are the four major factors in determining SAFE surfacing choices, a few other factors may also influence your final selection of surfacing materials. These include children's development, accessibility, and policy considerations.

Children's Development

The developmental stage of the children you serve must be taken into account: not all loose fill, for example, is suitable to every age. Two-year-olds will put pea gravel in their mouths and noses. Sand is so popular with preschoolers that they may prefer playing with it to playing with playground equipment, which means you may end up with less fill than needed around popular equipment. Wood chips can become weapons when wielded by older children; shredded rubber and wood chips can be doused with fuel and set on fire. As in most cases involving children, effective **supervision** is the key to maintaining SAFE playgrounds.

Accessibility

Accessibility for children with disabilities must be factored into your mix of surfacing materials. Pathways must be firm; stable; slip resistant (ASTM International F1951, 2014); wide enough for wheelchairs; and offer clear, unobstructed access from outside areas (for example, parking lots, walkways, school buildings, child care centers, or recreation centers) to the edge of playgrounds. Playgrounds do not need accessible surfacing throughout, but they must provide ways for children with disabilities to get to and onto ground-level or elevated equipment—for example, a rubber-tile pathway can lead to equipment, while wood chips can be used below the equipment.

Policy

Your program may share responsibility for the playground's fall surfaces with other groups. It is critical that responsibility for selection, installation, maintenance, and replacement of playground fill be spelled out and agreed upon before the surfaces are installed. Here, in a nutshell, are elements you must reach agreement on:

1. Responsibility for selecting surfacing materials: an agreement should spell out who will determine the appropriate surfacing material.
2. Responsibility for managing surfacing materials: an agreement must be reached on use zones and play equipment, since these determine how much and what kinds of surfacing materials will be used.

3. Responsibility for maintaining surfacing materials: an agreement should spell out who is responsible for maintaining and replacing surfacing materials.

4. Responsibility for training: an agreement should specify who provides and who receives training. We have observed new playground equipment with serious safety problems because maintenance staff were not trained to spot problems. (At a minimum, maintenance staff should be familiar with the latest edition of the CPSC's *Public Playground Safety Handbook.*)

5. Responsibility for inspecting surface materials: an agreement should specify who will inspect surface materials and how manufacturers' recommendations, ASTM International standards, and CPSC guidelines will be implemented.

6. Compliance with standards: be sure any surface materials you are purchasing comply with impact-attenuation standards, accessibility standards, age appropriateness, CPSC guidelines, and ASTM International F1292 and F1951 standards.

7. Product warranties and certifications: be sure products are protected for specified time periods by product warranties or certifications.

8. Accessibility: be sure pathways are accessible from outside the playground to the playground equipment.

How Much Does Surfacing Material Cost?

Cost is most organizations' first consideration when determining what kind of surfacing materials to buy. Resist the urge to view cost as merely the initial outlay: your real cost is likely to be quite different. The following formula gives you a more realistic way of looking at actual costs:

$$\frac{\text{initial cost} + \text{installation cost} + \text{yearly maintenance cost}^* = \text{true cost}}{10 \text{ years}}$$

*This should include replacement cost of loose fill.

Loose Fill: A Bargain?

At first glance, loose fill seems far less expensive than unitary surfacing. However, look more closely at its continuous cost, and it may not seem like such a bargain after all: loose fill can only be installed after dirt or other surfaces have been removed and trucked away; barriers must be put and kept in place to contain it; more fill must be periodically trucked in to replace the old; and continual maintenance is needed to rid loose fill of animal and insect feces, weeds, fungi, and other contaminants. Most loose fill also needs replenishing every year, regular sweeping or raking into place, and vigilant monitoring for foreign objects. If you add these expenses to the initial cost of loose fill, you'll find that your true cost may be 130 percent of the initial price of the fill. Once you've calculated these recurring costs, a decade's worth of loose fill may cost you about the same as unitary surfacing.

Unitary Surfacing: Too Expensive?

Unitary surfacing materials must be installed by professionals, so your initial cost for materials and installation can be ten times that for loose fill. However, unitary materials usually last about ten years, with minimum upkeep.

Table 4.4 is a brief overview of what you get from loose and unitary surfacing materials.

Other Installation Considerations

Several other factors should be considered when you're deciding on loose or unitary surfacing. These factors include your playground's slope and drainage and adequate coverage of the concrete footers that secure play equipment.

Slope

The slope of your playground may determine where you use unitary or loose-fill surfacing. Any fill at the base of a hill will receive drainage from that slope. Loose fill can be washed right over its containment barriers after heavy rains. When parking lots stand above the playground, oils and other vehicle contaminants may wash down onto the fill. In situations like these, loose fill is not a good choice. In more level areas, where the ground does not slope more than 1 percent, water may nonetheless pool in low spots. Unitary surfacing in level spots may need to be swept dry before children can use it.

Drainage

If a use zone cannot be drained adequately by elevating it, a gravel base should be used below loose fill. Typically, 2–3 inches (5–7.5 cm.) of gravel are installed as

Table 4.4. Selecting Playground Surfaces

Type of Material	Wheelchair Accessible	Maintenance Needed	Flammable	Cost	Initial Cost	Estimated 10-Year Cost	Professional Installation Required	Manufacturer Warranty Product Liability
Engineered wood fiber	Yes	Medium	Maybe	$$$	$$	$$$	Maybe	Yes
Pea gravel	No	High	No	$$	$$	$	No	No
Poured in place	Yes	Low	No	$$$	$$$	$$	Yes	Yes
Rubber mats/tiles	Yes	Low	Maybe	$$$	$$$	$$	Yes	Yes
Sand	No	No	No	$	$	$$	No	No
Shredded rubber	Maybe	Maybe	Medium	$$	$$	$$	No	Maybe
Wood chips	No	No	High	$	$	$$$	No	No

Figure 4.4. A post in its place before pouring the concrete that will secure it.

a base, a filter cloth is spread over the gravel, and then loose fill is added. Using this entire system is particularly important when wood products are the loose fill because water hastens their decomposition.

Covering Concrete Footers

SAFE play equipment is secured with large, upright posts that are held in their post holes by poured concrete (see fig. 4.4). The top of the concrete must be at least 6 inches (15.2 cm.) below the base of loose-fill materials. For example, if you are using wood chips with gravel and a filter cloth, then you would measure 6 inches (15.2 cm.) down from the filter cloth.

Slope, drainage, and placement of concrete footers are critical to the proper installation of loose-fill surfacing. All concrete footers should be at least 6 inches (15.2 cm.) under the ground surface. This will ensure that if the loose fill material is kicked out, no concrete will be showing. In addition, contrasting equipment pieces with the color of the surfacing may give a visual cue to children about possible tripping hazards. The best recommendation is to follow the manufacturer's installation requirements.

Routine Maintenance of Fall Surfaces

Finally, whatever your choices of fall-surfacing materials, they will not remain safe unless they are well maintained. The NPPS conducted studies in 2000 and 2004 that revealed fewer than 19 percent of all surveyed playgrounds maintained loose fill at depths adequate to cushion falls from play equipment. The problem was particularly critical around swings and slides (Hudson, Olsen, and Thompson 2004). Play equipment surrounded by sand, pea gravel, wood fill, or loose rubber fill may need daily maintenance (that is, the fill may need to be moved back beneath high-impact areas, such as swings and climbing structures).

Vandalism

Vandalism is cyclical. At Halloween, for example, razor blades and other sharp objects may appear on slides and in loose fill. During the summer months, when fewer school staff are around, school playgrounds may experience more vandalism. Vandalism also becomes more common on weekends, particularly holiday weekends, when parks are heavily used and large groups gather.

Incidents

The chief cause of incidents involving fall surfaces is inadequate depth of loose-fill materials. We have already discussed the relationship between falls from play structures; here, we call your attention to tripping accidents. The CPSC's guidelines identify the two most common causes of tripping accidents on playgrounds as exposed anchoring devices and barriers used to contain loose fill (fig. 4.5).

Containment barriers are commonly installed to prevent loose fill from being scattered throughout play areas. Make sure your barriers are highly visible by painting them colors that contrast vividly with the fill itself. Apply this color coding to changes in elevation too. One school nurse reported to the NPPS that the injury rate of children in her school was reduced by 95 percent after she painted the twelve stairs between one part of the playground and another a bright yellow to warn children of the change in elevation.

That clever nurse in the example above made intelligent use of accident reports to identify a problem and find a solution. Do the same, making regular use of your accident reports and maintenance checklists to routinely inspect fall surfaces. By doing so, you can identify problems and reduce accidents involving fall surfaces. (A routine inspection checklist is also available in appendix G.)

Figure 4.5. Exposed concrete footings are one of the two most common tripping accidents on playgrounds. Loose filling should rise at least 6 inches (15.2 cm.) above concrete footers to ensure it will not shift or be kicked away.

In 2004, a midsized parks and recreation department in Illinois was sued by the parents of an eight-year-old who had broken his arm while playing in the park. The parents alleged that the department had not properly maintained the surfaces under and around the play equipment. However, the department could document its policy for ongoing maintenance, which included weekly inspections. The depth of the loose fill in question had been checked the morning of the accident and had met the requirements. Depositions revealed that the child had leaped from an 8-foot- (2.4 m.) high platform during a game of tag and had landed awkwardly on the loose-fill surface. The investigation concluded that the cause of the boy's injury had more to do with his inappropriate behavior—playing tag on elevated equipment and jumping from it rather than sliding down—than with maintenance of the surfacing. Adequate documentation and good maintenance practices were critical in proving that the playground's surfacing was not the cause of the child's injury. The lawsuit was subsequently dropped.

Two lessons can be learned from this case: first, keeping good records can help you if a lawsuit occurs. Second, no matter how safe your surfacing is, injuries can still occur, depending on how children fall. SAFE practices don't prevent all injuries—rather, they minimize the number and severity of them.

Annual Assessments of Playground Safety

In addition to **routine maintenance** checklists and accident reports, each year you should compile an annual report consolidating routine information on all accidents and injuries involving fall surfaces. Doing so will help you identify potential hazards and dangerous features that need attention.

Keep all correspondence with manufacturers and distributors of surfacing materials indefinitely. These records may become critically important if your organization is a party to a lawsuit, because they document how you have worked with your vendors. A second reason to keep these records is that in many states, children can file lawsuits for up to two years after they have reached their majority. Keep your records of accidents, maintenance, and dealings with vendors for decades after playgrounds have been altered or removed.

In chapter 5, we will look more closely at the crucial role of maintenance in SAFE playgrounds.

Discussion Questions

1. Visit a local playground and examine the height of the play equipment. Can you identify different challenges associated with different heights of equipment, or are the challenges to children similar—for example, a 6-foot (1.8 m.) slide and an 8-foot (2.4 m.) slide?

2. Look at the surfaces below and around playground equipment. If the fill is loose, how many inches or centimeters deep is it? How high is the highest equipment? Is the surfacing you measured deep enough to cushion a fall from the highest equipment?

3. If the fill is unitary, is it free from foreign objects and loose toys? Is the surface free from holes? Can you tell if the surface is secured to a hard surface, such as cement or asphalt?

Chapter 5

SAFE Equipment Maintenance

Y ou have learned the importance of providing your playground with age-appropriate, accessible equipment and fall-absorbing surfaces. Without effective, systematic maintenance, however, those thoughtfully chosen swings, ladders, and surfacing materials cannot provide **SAFE** play for children.

This chapter focuses on the critical topic of maintenance. Slipshod maintenance can void manufacturers' warranties, put children in physical danger, waste dollars on unusable equipment, and open your organization to lawsuits when accidents occur.

A National Problem

Nearly 60 percent of all playground injuries that lead to litigation cite lack of maintenance as the primary cause of injury (Hendy 2004). Steve King's 1995 study revealed that one-third of the nine hundred park departments in his sample had never conducted a safety inspection of their equipment, despite almost half of it being more than ten years old (King 1995). We reached similar conclusions in the studies we conducted for the NPPS in 2000 and 2004 (Hudson, Mack, and Thompson 2000; Hudson, Olsen, and Thompson 2004).

Among the most common hazards identified:

- *Loose fill:* Loose fill under and around playground equipment was poorly maintained, particularly around swings and slides. Fewer than 19 percent of all playgrounds maintained loose fill at depths adequate to cushion falls from equipment.

- *Older play equipment:* Equipment installed before 1991 created far more problems (for example, gaps, head **entrapment**) than newer equipment. Older equipment may need more maintenance because of cumulative wear and tear. It may not be compliant with current **guidelines**—for instance, the **CPSC** guidelines were first published in 1981 and have since been updated in 1991, 1994, 1997, 2008, and 2010.

- *Materials hazards:* Thirty-five percent of wooden equipment contained splinters; 25 percent of metal equipment was rusty; 4 percent of plastic equipment was cracked. Protruding bolts (15 percent), missing parts (11 percent), and broken parts (26 percent) of equipment sampled suggest the breadth of playground maintenance problems. (For a complete summary of our findings by state, go to playgroundsafety.org.).

Standard of Care

As we discussed in chapter 2, *standard of care* is the legal term for the duty of public entities (for instance, early childhood programs, schools, community parks) to protect individuals against unreasonable risk of harm. Unless a public entity has been granted governmental immunity and cannot legally be sued, it is subject to lawsuits arising from charges of **negligent** behavior. Negligent behavior is conduct that doesn't reflect the standard of care that prudent professionals should provide. In the case of playground staff, this means subjecting children to unreasonable risks of injury. The law holds everyone to the same standard, whether maintenance staff, teacher, aide, or administrator: no one gets off the hook because of his or her job description. Ignorance is no defense in the eyes of the law.

In lawsuits involving equipment maintenance, the CPSC's guidelines are widely considered the minimum standard of care for playground equipment and surfacing. In most lawsuits, a program's staff will be held to the standard of care or **standards** of practice set forth in the CPSC's guidelines. You must remain up-to-date with these to protect children, yourself, and your organization.

The Importance of Comprehensive Maintenance and Playground Injuries

Inadequate maintenance is one of the most common factors in playground injuries, so you must develop truly comprehensive maintenance policies. Here is an example that illustrates how broad your conception of responsible maintenance must be—and the consequences of conceiving of it too narrowly.

One of us was asked to consult in a legal case in which a child on a Little League team was injured outside of the playing field. Alongside the field stood a jagged cement culvert, which paralleled the ball field's first baseline. No fencing or warning was present to warn children about the culvert. In what was clearly a case of foreseeable harm, a child chased a ground ball into the ditch where the culvert stood and hit his head on the jagged cement, resulting in a deep, 4-inch (10.1 cm.) gash on his forehead that required stitches and plastic surgery. Although the culvert wasn't part of the playing field, its proximity created a hazardous situation to the children on the playing field, and it was therefore the responsibility of the ball field's maintenance staff to protect children from the potential hazard. The agency ended up settling the lawsuit for a six-figure amount, far more than it would have cost to correct the problem in the first place.

Maintenance Planning

When you first start to plan a playground, the maintenance schedule should be part of that plan. A representative of the maintenance staff should be a member of your playground planning committee. Why? Because without the maintenance staff's valuable input, a playground is likely to fall into disrepair quickly. We have seen this happen repeatedly. Too often the recommendations of maintenance staff are not solicited or are offered but ignored, despite the fact that no one is better positioned to understand the durability of surfaces and equipment, how easy or difficult they are to maintain, and how much vandalism and abuse the playground is likely to sustain. Because maintenance staff members are directly responsible for maintaining safe play areas, they have a vested interest in those areas. Incorporate their suggestions into your plans, just as you incorporate maintenance into your playground.

Types of Maintenance

Your playground needs three kinds of maintenance: routine, remedial, and preventive. Each kind has specific objectives, and all are interrelated.

Routine Maintenance

The most frequent maintenance is routine. This may be done daily, weekly, or monthly to ensure that play areas are optimally safe and function smoothly. Routine checks or inspections should be made of equipment; surfaces; and supports such as walkways, shade, light fixtures, and fences. How often routine inspections are made depends on several factors: manufacturers' recommendations; equipment size and type; equipment age, frequency of use, and frequency of repairs; and materials used.

Manufacturers' Recommendations

Reputable manufacturers who subscribe to **ASTM International** standards and CPSC guidelines provide recommended inspection and maintenance routines for the equipment they sell. This information should form the framework of your inspection and maintenance program.

Equipment Size and Type

Large equipment with many nuts, bolts, and moving parts needs to be inspected more frequently than smaller, simpler structures. The more connecting parts the equipment has, the greater the possibility that a fastener or joint support may work itself loose during normal use. Unless they are checked and repaired frequently, such features can lead to **entanglement** or **entrapment**.

Equipment Age and Frequency of Repairs

Our 2000 and 2004 NPPS studies found that the older the equipment, the greater its maintenance problems (Hudson, Mack, and Thompson 2000; Hudson, Olsen, and Thompson 2004). Equipment lasts a long time if it is maintained regularly, yet the older it is, the more care it needs to remain safe and usable. We have found this is especially true of moving equipment, such as track rides, that has been on a playground for a long time. The bearings wear, or children place rocks or other objects in the track. Documenting the purchase dates of equipment can help you determine when it is time to replace it. Good record keeping will show you what kinds of equipment breaks down repeatedly. When repairs become needed more often, inspections should be conducted more often too.

Frequency of Use

How often equipment gets used is another factor affecting how often it needs to be checked or inspected for maintenance purposes. School playground equipment used daily by three hundred children, nine months a year, demands more frequent maintenance than city park equipment used by only fifty children on weekends. However, don't allow previous low-frequency use to lull you into lax or inconsistent maintenance. Don't omit inspections of school playgrounds during the summer just because school isn't in session, and don't ignore park playgrounds just because it is winter and cold outside. When equipment is available to children, they will use it.

Materials Used

Metal rusts, wood splinters, and plastic cracks—there is just no such thing as maintenance-free material. When rust builds up, it weakens metal parts, so it should be removed as quickly as possible. Wooden equipment needs to be treated every six to twelve months with preservatives to prevent splinters and dry rot. Plastic equipment should be inspected regularly for cuts, nicks, and cracks caused by heavy use or vandalism.

You can prevent or lessen material deterioration by choosing materials appropriate to your climate and frequency of use. For example, metal equipment doesn't do well in Hawaii because salt air corrodes it. Wooden equipment doesn't do well in hot climates because it dries out and splinters if not maintained meticulously.

If equipment is to be used every day or every weekend rather than once a month, make sure it is made of durable materials and is appropriate for heavy (daily) use. For instance, one of the problems we have found in early childhood programs is that their equipment is likely to have been bought at local discount distributors (such as Walmart, Target, or Home Depot) and is designed for home rather than public use. The materials these slides, swings, and climbing equipment are made of are less durable than equipment designed for public use because manufacturers assumed that only one or two children would be using them, not a whole group of children (six or more daily). Even with good maintenance, such equipment will not stand up to the constant wear and tear that occurs with multiple users. While these pieces bought at local discount distributors may be used by family care providers, they simply should not be present in child care programs open to public use.

Surfacing materials must also be maintained regularly (see chapter 4 for more details), especially loose fill, because it shifts around so much. Play areas using sand, pea gravel, wood products, or loose rubber fill may need daily maintenance to return fill to high-impact areas beneath swings and climbing structures.

Vandalism and Quality of Care

In areas where vandalism is common, playgrounds may need frequent inspections (see chapter 4 for information on vandalized **fall surfaces**). Besides restoring vandalized playgrounds to safe use, good maintenance may slow down or prevent some vandalism because of the psychological phenomenon known as *quality of use*: people's behavior in public spaces is affected by their perception of the upkeep and tidiness (or lack thereof) of their surroundings. The concept was first introduced in Beverly Driver's book *Elements of Outdoor Recreation Planning* and has been applied in parks and recreation work since the 1970s (Driver 1974). For instance, if you make use of a well-maintained picnic area in a park where litter has been picked up, trash containers are empty, and picnic tables are free of graffiti, you are more likely to leave the place as attractive as you found it. If the area is not well kept—litter strewn about, trash containers overflowing, names carved into tables— you are more likely to leave the area in as bad, if not worse, shape as you found it. (In recent years, quality of use has been used as a rationale for cities to keep empty buildings well maintained, lawns mowed, streetlights shining, and piled-up newspapers and mail removed from front porches in high-crime neighborhoods, and to fill empty shop windows with community displays. The perceived order and liveliness of well-tended cityscapes is thought to prevent vandalism and civic despair.)

Accidents

Accidents are inevitable on playgrounds. But effective, regular maintenance lessens their impact and creates a record of the equipment that is most often involved in them. For example, figure 5.1 shows a glider that was built for children who use wheelchairs. The reasons for installing the glider were admirable, but its execution of use left a lot to be desired: maintenance staff discovered that children who were not disabled were standing behind the glider and shoving it so hard that parts of it were breaking. Not only was this not the intended use of the equipment, but the children's acts turned the glider into a gigantic battering ram that could injure anyone in its path. Because maintenance staff spotted these problems during their routine inspections, they were able to modify the glider to prevent injuries and avoid potential lawsuits.

Figure 5.1. Glider for children using wheelchairs.

Similar to routine checks and inspections, accident reports help track problems. For instance, when 90 percent of reported injuries on a playground involve splinters, you can easily see that wooden equipment needs more frequent inspections and preventive maintenance. When one piece of equipment shows up time and again in accident reports, it is time to decide if it is appropriate for the site. To determine which equipment or materials cause accidents, routine inspection checklists like the one in table 5.1 should be used.

Table 5.1. Routine Inspection Checklist

Date: _____

EQUIPMENT

	Condition	Action Taken
Stability of handholds		
Sharp edges, splinters, rough surfaces		
Protrusions of nuts and bolts		
Wear and deterioration		
Rust and chipping paint		
Missing/broken parts		

Name _____

One caution about checklists: these are assets to you only if you use them effectively. Properly filled out and acted upon checklists can help you prove that your agency has been proactive in maintaining its playground. Suppose, for instance, that your maintenance policy states that an area is to be checked every three days. Say the area was last checked on Wednesday, and on Thursday an accident occurred there. In this instance, a checklist can attest to the fact that your agency possesses a safety maintenance program as well as prove the accident *was* indeed an accident and not the result of negligence.

Now suppose instead that a problem with the playground area was discovered on Wednesday, but no action was taken, and no record was made of preventing children from playing in the area on Thursday. When the accident occurs that day, your organization could be proven to have possessed foreknowledge of the problem and to have done nothing to prevent it.

To be useful, then, checklists must be carefully adapted to a particular site and used to propel appropriate, decisive, and recorded action. Otherwise, these lists are simply paperwork that gets filed away and that, with any luck, won't get used against your organization in a lawsuit.

Remedial Maintenance

Remedial maintenance is usually undertaken in response to problems found during routine maintenance inspections. Once a problem has been discovered, it needs to be taken care of, not simply noted. In essence, remedial maintenance consists of the actions triggered by routine maintenance inspections. If a repair is minor—say, adding loose fill under the swings—it should be completed immediately. If it isn't repaired immediately, a minor repair like a loose bolt can become a major one. The problem and its solution should also be recorded. Always describe the action taken to solve the problem (for example, *fixed, contacted main office, contacted manufacturer*). Recognizing a problem and failing to take action puts your organization in legal jeopardy if a child becomes injured.

If you can't repair a problem immediately, you must prevent children from using the equipment or area until you can fix it. Simply putting yellow tape around the broken or missing part is not sufficient. Yellow tape only serves to attract children to the problem area, where their natural curiosity prompts them to explore what the tape means. In inspecting the problem area, children could become injured or make the repair more difficult. When an area becomes off-limits, use fencing or other major barriers to keep children away from it.

Do Sweat the Small Stuff!

Make sure that maintenance staff always corrects the small stuff. Children have ways of discovering small problems—for instance, small tears in poured-in-place surfaces—and when they do, small problems often become much bigger ones.

Preventive Maintenance

Thorough equipment inspections should be completed at least once a year. This type of maintenance is much more detailed than routine maintenance. For instance, in routine maintenance, a staff member may quickly eyeball the top fasteners to make sure all bolts are in place. In preventive maintenance, the staff member will use a stepladder to actually inspect the collar of the fastener, as well as the nuts and bolts, to make sure they are not worn.

Preventive maintenance makes accidents like this one much less likely:

At a public park in Texas, the maintenance staff performed its routine inspections by driving by the park and eyeballing the equipment. Soon after, a twelve-year-old girl who was swinging on a swing at the park reached the highest point in the arc when the collar of the swing fastener broke. She suffered two broken legs. In depositions, the staff admitted that the wear and tear on the swing collar had never been inspected (and it takes a long time for steel collars to wear thin). An annual intensive inspection would have prevented injuries. The agency had no choice but to settle out of court for ten times what it would have cost to replace the swing collar.

During **preventive maintenance** inspections, all fasteners and chains (for instance, nuts and bolts, swing chains, S-hooks, and fasteners at the tops of swings), as well as areas where bolts are secured, should be inspected to ensure that they are still in place and not worn. Chipped paint should be removed and replaced with a fresh coat; wooden equipment should be treated with a preservative; and plastic equipment should be thoroughly inspected for nicks and cuts. Preventive maintenance can eliminate most causes of catastrophic incidents involving equipment failure.

The Importance of Original Parts

Most manufacturers provide purchasers of play equipment with detailed lists of parts. When you first buy equipment, order extra bolts and screws, fasteners, and other small parts that wear out and are needed for maintenance. If you don't, sometimes play equipment cannot be used for several months because one small part is back-ordered.

For equipment repairs, use *only* parts from the manufacturer. Using substitute parts you have purchased at the local hardware store can imperil children. Playground equipment and parts are manufactured to the exact specifications detailed in ASTM International F1487 or ASTM International F2373. Their tensile strength and durability meet the standards needed for safe use on each piece of equipment. Although a hardware store's parts may look the same, there is no guarantee that they meet ASTM International standards; they may be less durable or less reliable. You may be putting children's safety at risk by using these parts.

Use of third-party parts may also void manufacturers' warranties. Every manufacturer has its own specifications for swing chains, fasteners, seats, and other parts. If you decide to replace a broken swing chain with one made by a different manufacturer, you have now created a hybrid swing set. Neither the original manufacturer nor the manufacturer of the hardware store part will accept responsibility for the equipment from that point forward. Do not mix and match manufacturers' parts on one piece of equipment.

Preventing Major Playground Hazards

CPSC guidelines (2010) recommend that maintenance staff pay particular attention to seven equipment hazards when conducting routine maintenance checks and inspections. What these hazards are, where they are likely to be found, and what remedial actions should be taken to address them are described below.

Crushing and Shearing Points

Equipment that can "crush or shear limbs should not be accessible to children on a playground" (CPSC 2010, 14). Several varieties of equipment pose such threats, including merry-go-rounds, seesaws, rocking equipment, and moving equipment. Remedial action doesn't necessarily demand removal of such equipment, but it does call for removing their potential hazards. That means ensuring that no mechanisms that could crush any part of a child are accessible. Additionally, platforms shouldn't move up and down while they rotate—the distance between them and the ground should remain steady throughout rotation.

> One of us testified in a case in which a merry-go-round had been deliberately installed at an angle that left the platform 2 feet (0.6 m.) off the ground on the high side and 6 inches (15.2 cm.) from the ground on the low side. A five-year-old whose feet were dangling over the edge caught one foot under the low side of the platform as it spun, and his leg was crushed. The result was two severe breaks, several leg surgeries, and a major lawsuit.

Most seesaws now come equipped with spring fulcrums that allow up-down motion but prevent crushing points. These more modern pieces prevent one side of the seesaw from dropping suddenly when the child opposite gets off the seat. This newer equipment also prevents back and neck injuries.

Spring rockers, another favorite in early childhood play areas, now come equipped with recoiled springs that prevent crushing. Some manufacturers have redesigned spring rockers so only a continuous, pliable length of metal is used.

Entanglement and Impalement

Entanglement occurs when protruding parts of equipment snare the clothing, drawstrings, shoelaces, hair, or jewelry worn by children. Potential entanglements must be repaired immediately, as strangulation from entanglement is the leading cause of death in play areas. It is important maintenance staff and caregivers (teachers, aides) work together to accomplish these immediate repairs.

Bolts and fasteners (S-hooks, C-hooks) are the most easily spotted entanglements identified by maintenance staff. S-hooks are particularly dangerous because once they start to separate, only an expensive tool and major effort can close the gap effectively. According to one CPSC report, "a hook is considered closed when there is no gap or space greater than 0.04 inches (0.1 cm.), about the thickness of a dime" (2010, 12). Instead of S-hooks, many equipment manufacturers are now using clevises that screw closed to fasten swings.

Caregivers should not allow children who are wearing jewelry, mittens connected by strings, or upper-body clothing with drawstrings on play equipment. It takes less than thirty seconds for children under the age of five to lose consciousness when a string, rope, or hood catches them beneath their necks. In less than two minutes, they stop breathing.

Playground supervisors and aides should "remove any ropes, dog leashes, or similar objects that have been attached to playground equipment" (CPSC 2010, 14), as children can become entangled and strangle in these items. Similarly, maintenance staff should ensure ropes on play equipment are secured at both ends. This is especially critical at child care centers whose owners have bought equipment intended for home use—many of these structures come with unsecured climbing ropes.

Long bolts and unprotected round handholds (generally found on spring rockers) can cause **impalements**. Bolts should not protrude more than two threads from the ends of nuts (CPSC 2010). When bolts protrude by more than two threads, they can impale children who are running under equipment and not watching where they are going. Impalement can also occur when protruding spring-rocker handholds are not protected by cups. These handholds, generally found on older equipment, are at eye level for small children.

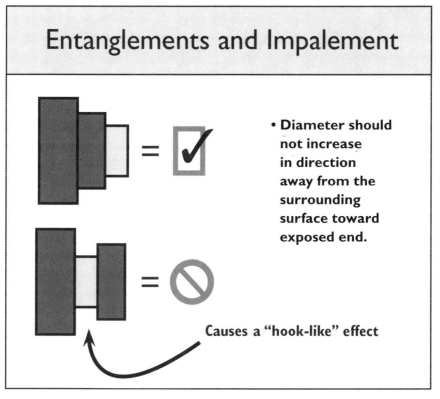

Figure 5.2. Problem area: hook

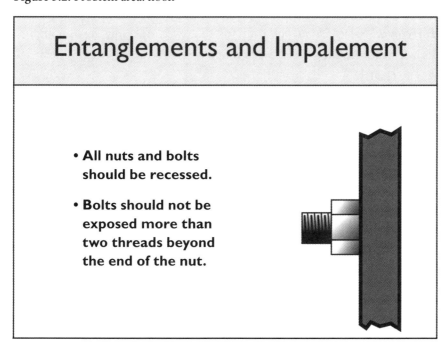

Figure 5.3. Problem area: nuts and bolts

Entrapment

Openings that can impede children from withdrawing their bodies, heads, or limbs can entrap them (CPSC 2010). When children can't remove their feet, arms, or clothing from an opening in a play structure, they can become very frightened. When their heads become trapped, they may die. Their heads can become entrapped whether children enter openings head or feet first. Headfirst entrapments commonly occur when young children insert their heads through openings in one direction, turn them in another direction, and then find themselves unable to back out of the openings. Because their cognitive abilities are limited, these young children are unable to figure out that simply by returning their heads to the original position, they can withdraw. Instead, they panic, increasing the likelihood that they will become entrapped and asphyxiated.

The chief factor leading to feet-first entrapments is the size of a young child's body in relation to their head. Until about age five, children's heads have a greater diameter than their bodies. When they sit or lie down on their stomachs and slide feet-first through openings, their bodies can slide through, but often not their heads. Entrapment can occur in openings with diameters between 3.5 to 9 inches (8.9 to 22.9 cm.). These include openings such as the spaces between decks and platforms, the guardrails on equipment manufactured before 1994, and wooden or metal ladders not manufactured to ASTM International standards. The CPSC's *Public Playground Safety Handbook* cautions that even openings low enough so children's feet can touch the ground may present risks of strangulation to entrapped children (CPSC 2010).

Children can also become entrapped in partially bound openings, such as those formed by two or more playground parts. V-shaped openings are found on picket fences and at the tops of certain old metal slides. To prevent entanglement on this type of equipment, its openings should be modified to form angles wider than 55 degrees (CPSC 2010).

Sharp Points, Corners, and Edges

The range of objects that can cut or puncture children's skin is vast. These objects include exposed ends of tubing, wooden materials, steel edges, and steel-belted tires used on tire swings, among other things. Regular preventive maintenance is needed to keep such equipment safe.

All exposed ends of tubing not resting on the ground should be capped or plugged, and the devices used to close them should not be removable, except with tools. All wooden parts should be smooth and splinter-free. Metal and wood corners should be rounded, and metal edges should be rolled or finished with rounded caps.

CPSC guidelines specify that slides should not have sharp edges (2010). Pay special attention to the metal edges on the sides and exits of slides. If steel-belted radial tires are used as playground climbing equipment, examine them closely and regularly to ensure that no steel belts or wires are exposed.

Suspended Hazards

Children can become injured when they run into or trip over cables, wire ropes, and other flexible equipment suspended above the ground. Parts that are suspended above the ground at an angle of 45 degrees or less and fewer than 7 feet (2.1 m.) above a protected surface should be considered suspended hazards. Keep all such parts away from high-traffic areas, and paint them bright or contrasting colors so they stand out from surrounding equipment and surfaces. Make sure these suspended parts can't loop back on themselves or onto other ropes, cables, or chains to form loops 15 inches (38.1 cm.) or wider. (Two adult fists should not be able to pass through a loop.) Additionally, suspended parts should always be fastened at both ends, unless they are 7 inches (17.8 cm.) or shorter or attached to swing seats (CPSC 2010).

Tripping Hazards

Tripping is most often occasioned by a sudden change in elevation. As stated in chapter 4, the CPSC identifies the most common elements in playground tripping accidents as protruding anchoring devices and barriers used to contain loose fill. The first of these hazards is definitely a maintenance problem; the second is a design *and* maintenance problem.

All anchoring devices for play equipment, such as concrete footings and horizontal bars at the base of flexible climbers, should be installed below ground level and covered by at least 6 inches (15.2 cm.) of surfacing fill materials. Deep fill ensures that even when loose material gets kicked out, the anchoring devices will not protrude to trip children.

When wooden or rubber barriers have been installed to contain loose fill, make sure they are visible. In too many cases, wood chips are piled up flush with the top of landscaping rails. While such barriers may keep 12 inches (30.5 cm.) of wood chips inside an area, they fail to alert children to the barriers' presence. Paint barriers so their color contrasts vividly with the fill so children can distinguish where one ends and the other starts.

Other Hazards

Worn tires are often recycled as flexible climbers, swing seats, or cushioning beneath seesaws. More recently, they have been shredded and sold as loose fill. When tires are present on your playground in any of these capacities, follow these CPSC (2010) guidelines to maintain them:

1. Steel-belted radials should be closely examined regularly to ensure that there are no exposed steel belts or wires.
2. Tires should be regularly drained and cleaned out so water and debris don't accumulate in them.
3. Shredded tire mulch "should be inspected before installation to ensure that all metal has been removed" (17).

What Maintenance Records Should We Create and Keep?

Record all playground maintenance inspections, checklists, and repairs. Create files for manufacturers' maintenance guidelines and correspondence with manufacturers' representatives, distributors, and other service providers. Create spreadsheets for each play area to document accidents and injuries there. Cumulatively, these documents can help you better understand how your organization works with playground vendors: for instance, if your organization has not worked well with a vendor to solve problems satisfactorily, you will know that hereafter you should contact the manufacturer directly. Such correspondence can also help you foresee potential problems involving ordering or buying new equipment and can be of great use should your organization be sued. Maintenance records will also help you identify potential hazards and dangerous features that warrant increased attention.

Table 5.4. Sample documentation checklist

For each play area under your jurisdiction, keep these documents on file.

Document	Date Filed	Comments
GENERAL INFORMATION		
Planning meeting minutes		
Initial letters for bid		
Acceptance contract		
Invoice		
Equipment warranty		
Site plan/construction dates		
Itemized list and quantity of play components		
Parts list		
Initial safety audit		
Inspection history checklists		
Remedial action history (work orders)		
Incident reports (injury, vandalism)		
Other		
Other		

From *SAFE and Fun Playgrounds: A Handbook* by Heather M. Olsen, EdD, Susan D. Hudson, PhD, and Donna Thompson, PhD, © 2016. Published by Redleaf Press, www.redleafpress.org.

Table 5.5. For each play area under your jurisdiction, document and keep a record of the following manufacturer information.

Document	Date Filed	Comments
MANUFACTURER'S INFORMATION		
Contact information		
Correspondence with manufacturer		
Manufacturer's compliance letters (certificates for ASTM International, CPSC, IPEMA)		
Manufacturer's installation drawings and instructions		
Manufacturer's installation verification		
Other:		
Other:		

From *SAFE and Fun Playgrounds: A Handbook* by Heather M. Olsen, EdD, Susan D. Hudson, PhD, and Donna Thompson, PhD, © 2016. Published by Redleaf Press, www.redleafpress.org.

As mentioned in chapter 4, these records need to be kept longer than the equipment itself, because in many states, children can file lawsuits for up to two years after they reach their majority. Because of this, it is imperative you have access to all of these records for more than ten years or so—possibly even closer to two decades.

Tables 5.4 and 5.5 provide a sample checklist of the records you must keep on file. (This sample checklist is also available for photocopying in appendix H.)

Planning for Maintenance: Annual Budget Requests

Compiling annual budget requests and setting aside monies for maintenance and repair should be part of your overall maintenance plan. A good rule of thumb is to allocate at least 10 percent of the original cost of play equipment each year for repair materials. Having these monies available means that you can make repairs when they're needed and save any surplus to defray the cost of future replacements. With faithful maintenance, most play equipment bought today is likely to last fifteen to twenty years.

Appendix G provides you with a comprehensive, routine inspection checklist. Consult it when you are planning your maintenance budgets.

Discussion Questions

1. Choose a local park and a local child care facility's play area, and use the basic checklist (table 5.1) to assess the condition of the equipment you find there. If you can, find out the frequency of routine maintenance on each playground.
2. Visit three local child care facilities' play yards and see if you can determine whether the equipment there is designed for home or public use. If you know or can approach administrators, ask what criteria their organization uses in selecting equipment for their play areas.

Chapter 6

Planning Your SAFE Playground

Children need a variety of play—motor and physical, social, constructive, fantasy, rule-bound—because play is "the most efficient, powerful, and productive way to learn the information young children need" (Wardle 2008). Playgrounds should be designed so children can explore, gratify their curiosity, and express themselves physically.

How do you create or remodel a playground that is fun, challenging, and safe for children; affordable; easy to supervise; as easy to maintain as you can make it; and attractive to staff, children, parents, and the surrounding community? Just how do you go about turning this vision into reality?

The short answer is effective planning. You—and this is a collective *you*, because many people will be involved—need to anticipate as many contingencies as possible: funding, designing, siting, equipping, providing access, constructing, and maintaining your playground. You need to reach consensus about who is responsible for what among the many players in this elaborate game. When you approach creating a **SAFE** playground this way, you will encounter fewer surprises; you will be able to spend more of your time and energy on the components of SAFE play: **supervision**, age-appropriateness, effective **fall surfaces**, and adequate equipment maintenance. You will spend less time putting out unexpected fires.

What Not to Do

Playgrounds that are built with goodwill but without careful planning are unlikely to work well for the children who use them, the people who maintain them, the people who supervise their use, and the organizations that fund them. If you have read our previous chapters, you know that an almost limitless number of things can go wrong.

The Hudson Memorial Church decided to open a child care center for members' children. Because of the limited budget, church administrators asked parishioners to donate play equipment for the new playground. Volunteers fenced off a grassy, sunny area near the classroom building for the playground. They filled it with plastic play equipment, much of it donated from members' backyards. They dug a pit for a sandbox and erected an old backyard swing set.

Within six months, administrators needed to close the playground because of a lengthy list of problems: too many minor injuries from collisions, too many cuts from cracked plastic equipment, and one major fall. By then, the sandbox had developed drainage problems, and the sand was contaminated by cat feces. Clearly, the playground had become a liability rather than an asset.

As one exasperated parent remarked, "I thought children's outdoor play was supposed to be fun, not work for the adults."

That parent quoted in the story about the Hudson Memorial Church was right: a playground *is* supposed to be fun. But setting up and maintaining one also involves lots of work for adults. When the people who create a playground fail to plan sufficiently—when they simply fence off an area, fill it with donated equipment, and hope for the best—then the truly hard work will fall to supervisors, maintenance staff, and administrators. Don't let this happen to your program.

What We Know Works

At the NPPS, we have observed and participated in many plans for developing or renovating playgrounds, and we have used that experience to devise a planning process that works for most organizations. This chapter takes you through the sequence that we know leads to SAFE playgrounds.

Briefly, the crucial steps are determining the following:

- the ages of children your playground will serve
- the number of supervisors you will need (more detailed information on supervision can be found in chapter 2)

- the fall surfaces that work best for your site (we cover these considerations in detail in chapter 4)
- the level and kind of maintenance that play equipment must receive to remain safe (much more about this can be found in chapter 5)

Some of these steps must be taken before you design the playground, some during the design or development phase, and others after the playground has been built (see fig. 6.1) (NPPS 2000).

We realize that many agencies and organizations already have policies in place to cover planning from beginning through end. If yours does not, or you haven't planned to build or retrofit a SAFE playground before, you may benefit from the following recommendations. They are based on what we have observed in scores of cases.

The Planning Process

PREDESIGN
(Where are we going?)

DESIGN
(How are we going to get there?)

DEVELOPMENT
(Getting to the destination)

IMPLEMENTATION/EVALUATION
(Where did we go?)

Figure 6.1.

Predesign Phase

Timeline: three to six months

The predesign phase is the back-office phase of your plan. During this time, you will make those determinations that give specific shape to your collective vision: what ages of children your playground will serve; how big the playground will be; how many supervisors you will need; how your climate and site may affect layout and play equipment; and who will be responsible for maintaining the site, and how.

Forming a Planning Committee

The first step of the predesign phase is forming your planning team. Playgrounds need the experience and perspectives of more than one individual if they are going to be effective and SAFE. The NPPS recommends your planning committee consist of six to ten people. If you have fewer than six members, chances are you aren't including all the individuals who have unique insight into the practicalities of the play areas (for example, maintenance personnel, frontline teachers, school nurses, supervisors). On the other hand, we have observed that groups larger than ten have more difficulty making decisions. If more than ten people want to get involved, you can divide the group into smaller, more manageable subcommittees.

Selecting an effective range of planning committee members is important. Here are our suggestions:

Child care center: several teachers, the director, a custodian, some board members, parents, and playground supervisors

Home child care: owner, provider, assistant provider, parent

School: upper and lower elementary teachers, including special education and physical education; administrator; outdoor play supervisor; school nurse; custodian; a representative from the PTO; chairperson for fundraising

Park or other community setting: parks and recreation director or park supervisor, maintenance staff, board member, city council member, program specialist, parents

It is important for supervisors to be involved in the design and layout of play areas. Their insights on safe sight lines, children's movement and behavior, separation of active and passive activities, and a suitable number of playthings can help avoid conflicts and unsafe behavior. In the case of schools and ECE programs, teachers, teaching associates and assistants, nurses or health educators, maintenance staff, and parents or caregivers should also be part of planning playground supervision.

Shaping the committee is also critical. Here are our suggestions:

Chair: runs meetings, helps to coordinate the committee's work and moves it toward consensus

Secretary: keeps notes of meetings and rosters of people who attended

Consultants: We recommend that consultants be invited to attend the first or second planning meeting. Unless committee members are uncommonly knowledgeable, it is useful to have someone familiar with playground design to help shape your committee's discussions. Playground equipment manufacturers and distributors may volunteer to help your committee, but they have vested interests in the advice they offer. Neutral consultants will serve you better. They are likely to charge a fee for their work, but they will save you money in the end. And your predesign committee may find the input of a neutral design consultant invaluable. The National Program for Playground Safety (http://playgroundsafety.org) can help you find neutral consultants.

What Should the Predesign Planning Committee Address?

The predesign committee should address the playground's purpose, the playground's intended activities, the playground's users, and the playground's hours.

The Playground's Purpose

The purpose of a playground may seem overly simple and obvious, but it is not. Outdoor playgrounds serve a variety of needs, and your first step should be to decide on the needs your own space will satisfy. Determining this will help you shape the actual space (Moore, Goltsman, and Iacofano 1987).

If your program is school or early childhood education (ECE) based, then a playground is likely to come with pedagogical strings attached: it may need, for example, to bring an indoor curriculum outdoors, or it may need to teach ecological lessons or apply classroom concepts to outdoor spaces. In these cases, elaborate play equipment may not be necessary. In a community (parks and recreation) playground, on the other hand, the overall aim is likely to be increasing children's physical fitness, in which case play equipment may be critical—particularly equipment that encourages children to do a lot of climbing. Additionally, some community playgrounds may be intended to foster cooperative social play, and these are designed differently than ones aimed at physical fitness.

When a predesign committee does not answer the fundamental question of a playground's purpose, it is likely to produce what we call ***succotash syndrome***—an uncoordinated batch of play elements stuck randomly in place.

The Playground's Intended Activities

While the purpose of your playground may be to teach cooperation or physical fitness or to connect children with the natural world, those are general goals. Planning for the playground's intended activities is much more specific. For example, an elementary school is likely to view its playground's purpose as the promotion of physical fitness—but what *sorts* of physical fitness? Perhaps you will define this as developing upper-body and arm strength. If this is the case, then the playground's design and equipment should focus on providing activities that strengthen children's upper bodies and arms.

The Playground's Users

In chapter 3, we discussed the importance of age-appropriate design, and in one sense, we put the cart before the horse in doing so: before you can design a SAFE playground, you first must decide on the age range of children it is intended to serve.

Establish age ranges as quickly as possible. The intended playground-user age may include several ranges, for example: six to twenty-three months, two to five years, and five to twelve years. When this is the case, decide who the primary users for each play area within the playground will be: don't simply plan to use smaller-scaled equipment for younger children in the same area where older children will play on bigger equipment.

Once you have designated age ranges, you can quickly eliminate certain categories of equipment. See the sample checklist on page 95 of items to keep out of toddler and preschool playgrounds.

Keep These Out of Toddler and Preschool Playgrounds

- overhead hanging rings
- trapeze rings
- pea gravel
- rope swings
- rope climbers that aren't secured at both ends
- merry-go-rounds
- track rides
- trampolines
- fulcrum seesaws
- ring treks
- vertical sliding poles
- arch climbers
- chain or cable walks
- free-standing climbing structures with flexible parts
- horizontal and rung ladders

The Playground's Hours

Before you can choose the right equipment to be bought and maintained, your committee needs to decide on the hours of likely use. For instance, will the hours be unstructured—that is, open for use all the time? Will the hours of use include before and after school time, or during school time only? And will the playground be supervised during any or all of the hours of use?

Answering these initial questions is important because the amount and the nature of anticipated use plays a big part in how you design and outfit a SAFE playground. Say your playground is part of an ECE program and will be used only when the program is in session. It will then, by definition, be closely supervised.

This means its equipment and surfacing won't need to be as hardy as those used in a neighborhood park where supervision isn't provided, equipment is available 24/7, and vandalism can easily occur. If your playground will be at a school that is open to the community after school hours, you should site the play equipment away from school buildings to prevent people from entering the building and wandering open hallways of the school.

Guidelines and Standards to Factor into Planning

Besides your own organization's preferences, you will probably need to factor in the **guidelines** and **standards** of other organizations or government agencies. ECE playgrounds in licensed facilities are one example. These playgrounds must follow state and professional guidelines for outdoor areas: for instance, their fences must be at least 4 feet (1.2 m.) high surrounding all play areas (NAEYC 2014). Table 6.1 summarizes the guidelines and standards that may be applicable to your playground.

Only after researching guidelines and standards and discussing and agreeing on answers to the basic questions of planning a playground should your committee proceed to the next planning phase: **site analysis**.

Table 6.1. Guidelines and Standards Applicable to SAFE Playgrounds

Organization	Website	Brief Description	Appropriate Public Agency
Americans with Disabilities Act (ADA)	www.access-board.gov	The ADA develops minimum guidelines and requirements for standards issued under the ADA and the Architectural Barriers Act.	Early childhood programs Schools Communities
American Society for Testing and Materials (ASTM) International	www.astm.org	ASTM International has developed voluntary guidelines for a variety of equipment and elements that are present in the outdoor environment (see chapter 3).	Early childhood programs Schools Communities
Consumer Product Safety Commission (CPSC)	www.cpsc.gov/ cpscpub/pubs/325.pdf	CPSC has issued voluntary guidelines for the use of public playgrounds. Guidelines present safety information for public playground equipment. The purpose of the CPSC guidelines is to address the hazards that result in playground-related injuries and deaths.	Early childhood programs Schools Communities
National Association for the Education of Young Children (NAEYC)	www.naeyc.org	Standard 9 of the 10 NAEYC accreditation standards, the Physical Environment standard, addresses safe and healthful environments that provide appropriate and well-maintained indoor and outdoor physical environments.	Early childhood programs Schools (pre-K)

Table 6.1. Guidelines and Standards Applicable to SAFE Playgrounds, cont.

Organization	Website	Brief Description	Appropriate Public Agency
National Health and Safety Performance Standards (NHSPS)	http://nrckids.org/ CFOC3/PDFVersion/ list.html	The NHSPS standards are published jointly by the American Public Health Association (APHA) and the American Academy of Pediatrics (AAP).	Early childhood programs Schools (pre-K)
National Clearinghouse for Educational Facilities (NCEF)	www.ncef.org	NCEF is a nongovernment, nonprofit organization authorized by Congress to provide information on designing, building, and maintaining safe, healthy, high-performing schools from early childhood and K–12.	Early childhood programs Schools (pre-K)

Site Analysis

The planning committee should now make an on-site inspection of the proposed playground area. Do this even if members are already familiar with it, because this time they will be looking at it through very different eyes. Arm them with a scaled map to inform their decision making. The map should include existing boundaries, easements, roads, buildings, waterways, high-tension wires, and other structures, as well as topographic features and climatological patterns that may affect the playground (Sawyer 2009).

The Environment

Make sure that the planning committee makes use of existing records of the proposed site, including the following:

Topographic maps and aerial photos. These records can be found in local libraries and can be used to identify slopes, drainage patterns, and other physical features.

Soil and Water Conservation District. This agency can provide data on soil composition, vegetation, and water-table levels.

National Weather Service. This agency can provide data on prevailing winds, temperatures, and other weather patterns.

Equipped with these data, your planning committee can then consider the suitability of the proposed site. The **site analysis** should next include examining these factors:

- *Soil and geology.* Soil type is important to drainage patterns. Hardpan, clay, compacted, or eroded soil, for example, creates ongoing drainage problems that can interfere with providing appropriate fall surfaces around play equipment.
- *Drainage.* Good drainage is one of the most critical factors in developing a SAFE and successful playground (fig. 6.2). Water should drain away from play areas. If you have noted that rainfall does not flow naturally away from the site, you may need to grade surfaces or install underground drainage lines to make the site usable. If the site is near a river, stream, or other body of water, consult a floodplain map to verify the playground will not lie inside the floodplain.

Figure 6.2. Poor drainage can occur when soil erodes or the earth beneath equipment becomes packed, like beneath these swings. In addition to regular upkeep of loose fill, a graded surface or an underground drainage system can help improve drainage.

- *Slope.* Areas where permanent play equipment is to be installed should have slopes of no more than 1–4 percent (a 1 percent slope rises 1 foot for every 100 linear feet, or 0.3 meters for every 30.5 meters). Areas with slopes of less than 1 percent may pose drainage problems because water will simply sit on their surfaces until it evaporates or freezes. Slopes greater than 4 percent may need to be graded before equipment and surfacing can be safely installed. To be accessible to users with physical disabilities, playgrounds can have slopes of no more than 5 percent across one axis and no more than 2 percent across the cross-axis.
- *Vegetation.* Every playground needs shade, especially playgrounds for ECE programs. Trees provide excellent shade and should be used on the south and west sides of a site. If your inspection reveals that the site cannot support trees to protect children from heat, you will need to substitute porous shade

structures above play equipment in place of trees in order to guard against heat-related injuries (see fig. 6.3).

Avoid use of messy or poisonous plants. Young children are drawn to bright, inedible berries and may eat them. Avoid planting or retaining trees that produce nuts or that send down endless leaves or branches (for example, silver maples), seasonally or in high winds because they will prove to be maintenance headaches.

- *Climate- and weather-related factors.* Sun and wind may affect where you choose to site play structures. Make sure you have allowed room to install equipment so it can face north or east when possible; check with local meteorologists to learn about prevailing winds and other climatic conditions that might affect your site. Don't install impermeable structures to shelter children from heat and direct sunshine, as these types of structures actually retain and intensify heat.
- *Existing structures.* Note on the site map as well as during the on-site inspection any structures or permanent features such as roads, utility lines, and ball fields. These will affect where you can place new equipment and

Figure 6.3. A shade structure.

structures—for example, you wouldn't want to place slides and swings directly across from a parking lot or a baseball diamond, because small children are inattentive to nearby traffic and games. You would not want to place play equipment on the opposite side of a road from restrooms, either.

Take note of any existing play equipment that doesn't meet current **CPSC** and **ASTM International** guidelines and standards; it will need to be removed, and the cost of removal and disposal must be factored into the cost of developing the site.

• *Nearby land use:* Investigate how nearby land is being used. Adjacent property may contribute unacceptable or unsafe noise, traffic, pollution, or other hazardous conditions. Check local building codes and property records to find out who owns nearby land and what agencies have authority over planning and zoning for them—you wouldn't want to build a playground only to discover that a new roadway, gas station, or wind farm is going in next door.

Utility easements should also be identified, even when nothing is presently built on the space. Easements give utility companies the right to install and maintain power lines; these could eventually disrupt the operation of your playground.

• *Hazardous conditions:* Identify any natural hazardous conditions present on the proposed site. These include ponds, streams, poisonous plants, and trees that shed pods, seeds, leaves, or branches heavily. Human-made hazardous conditions include utility lines, roadways, railroad tracks, ditches, and heavy-duty power lines. Do not develop playgrounds beneath power lines.

Finally, establish how you will evaluate the playground you build and the procedures that you used to create it. Questions the planning committee may want to ask during this evaluation may include:

• Does the playground reflect the planning goals?
• Are the children using the playground as expected?
• Does the area contribute to the development (for instance, physical, intellectual, emotional, social) of the children as anticipated?

Having this set of agreed-upon criteria to use when assessing the built playground will help you keep on track during the next two phases, design and building.

Table 6.2. Activity Analysis for Developing Manipulative Skills in an Early Childhood Education Playground

Activity description	Children will be able to use loose parts to dig, sift, and move sand materials.
User profiles	Toddlers and preschoolers will be primary users. These groups may or may not be steady on their feet, so easy entrance/exit into the area is a must.
Resource/facility requirements	The area should be level and accommodate ten children at one time. If ground level, it should have a containment barrier; if elevated, it should be no higher than x feet / meters and have accessible pathway and clearance.
Support factors	A storage area is needed nearby to house shovels, buckets, and other loose parts. The playground area should be shaded. Its surface (sand) needs to be covered when not in use.

Design Phase

Timeline: average of twelve to eighteen months

Now it is time to decide on the specific **activity centers** for the playground, search through catalogs for equipment ideas, and select the equipment and surfaces for each activity center. We suggest you obtain several copies each of anywhere between five to ten equipment and five to ten surfacing companies' product catalogs. When choosing products from these catalogs, don't base your choices on personal opinion; base them on the goals and objectives you defined during the predesign phase.

Designate Activity Centers

Activity centers are dedicated to specific play activities—for example, nature, ball games, dramatic play, or climbing. Your playground may include one or many such centers. The planning committee should designate each activity on its site map so that the possible interactions of different activities become visible. Doing this helps you group together activities such as musical games, dance, and drama in one area. It also allows you to easily spot potential user conflicts—for example, siting swing sets and a slide between two baseball diamonds. Breaking down playground space into activity zones will help prevent traffic problems, injuries, and congestion.

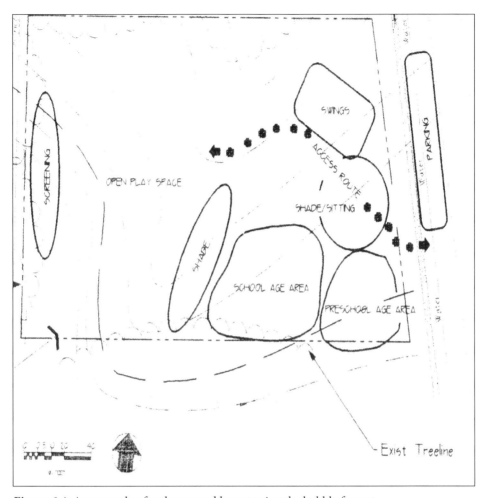

Figure 6.4: An example of a playground layout using the bubble format.

Conduct Activity Analysis

We have already discussed the importance of determining the purpose, use, and users of your SAFE playground. Now it is time to make sure that you have planned for the necessary resources, services, and support in order for your vision to become a reality. An **activity analysis** ensures that your activity centers have the resources needed to help children play SAFE. See table 6.2 for a sample analysis.

Lay Out the Playground

Begin laying out the playground on paper. Factor in all of the information you have gathered during your site analysis. Use a **bubble format** (see fig. 6.4) and a scaled site map; add the boundaries, access points, existing structures, hazards, shade, and other determinants. Bubbles represent where you want to locate each of the activity centers and pieces of equipment. A visual showing all of these things combined helps you see how the different components will fit together—or won't. You'll see where conflicts might occur and where play equipment and activity centers can best be sited in relation to gates, roads, paths, and buildings.

Create a Playground Budget

Every project operates within budget constraints; estimating costs at this phase will help you prioritize your spending on the playground. Having a budget in place for specific equipment or materials will also help you with fundraising because donors are more likely to help pay for something tangible (for instance, a swing set, a climbing tower) than for the vaguer "new or upgraded play area."

The committee should start by estimating costs for these items:

- site preparation
- equipment
- appropriate fall surfacing
- support amenities, such as water source, garden, fencing, lighting, storage units, entry and exit areas
- consulting fees (landscape architect, designer)

Developmental Phase

Timeline: average of twelve to eighteen months

Once a budget has been approved, your SAFE playground moves from a project on paper to a project on the ground.

Design and Construction Drawings

Design and construction drawings might be created by manufacturers of equipment or surfacing. They might also be produced in-house by your project committee or by a local architectural consulting firm. Construction drawings should show where the equipment, activity areas, use zones, entries and exits, pathways, and plantings are to be located. You may also want to hire a landscape designer to ensure plants chosen for the playground are appropriate.

Final Design Approval

The planning committee, owner, or administrator of the playground should provide final approval of the construction drawings. Approval should be made only after evidence and documentation of the following have been provided:

- compliance of equipment with stated uses and purposes
- compliance of equipment with applicable standards and guidelines
- compliance of activity centers and equipment with the ADA's accessibility and circulation requirements
- adequate and compliant surfacing under and around elevated play equipment
- appropriate amenities and safety structures, such as trees, water fountains, and fences
- documented proof of licenses and insurance or bonds by equipment installers
- documented liability insurance from equipment and surfacing manufacturers
- documented product warranties from equipment and surfacing manufacturers

Construction Timeline

The construction timeline is highly variable because the scale, ambition, complexity, and resources available to each SAFE playground vary so greatly. If the cost of construction is a big constraint, phased development and fundraising may make the most sense for your project. Be sure to build in enough time for unforeseeable delays, such as bad weather.

Installation of Equipment, Pathways, Shade Trees, and Amenities

Manufactured playground equipment must be installed according to its manufacturer's specifications; these must be provided in the form of clear and concise instructions (ASTM International F1487) for each structure. Instructions should include the manufacturer's recommendations or specifications for the following elements:

- use-zone placement of equipment
- depth of support posts
- method of mixing adhesives for surfacing
- ratio of cement to water
- proper tools and techniques for locking structural joints
- maintenance schedules (if your playground's maintenance schedule is more rigorous, you can use yours instead)

The manufacturer must also provide a complete parts list, which should be kept on file indefinitely (see chapter 5 for more details on the importance of record keeping). A manufacturer should also provide warnings, either in the form of labels on the equipment itself or in other formats. Most equipment labels caution about the needed depth of surfacing or the importance of active supervision when the equipment is in use. Posting and maintaining such warning labels helps adults supervise children more effectively and prevents children from being injured. Once these warning labels become illegible or are destroyed or removed, your program is responsible for replacing them. It is easiest to buy replacement labels when you order the equipment. This way the labels are available when you need to post them on equipment or signs describing the age levels for which equipment is suitable and the need for adult supervision. These signs are critical to include in playgrounds that will be used when schools are not in session. They should be posted outside the relevant play areas.

Who Will Install the Equipment and Surfacing?

Who is going to install the equipment and surfacing you purchase? Most often, programs use contractors recommended by manufacturers and distributors. Make sure installers have been trained by the manufacturer or are certified installers of playground equipment; certification should be with the International Playground Contractors Association, whose website maintains a list of certified playground installers for each state (www.playground-contractors.org).

When money is tight, many programs decide to use their own maintenance staff to install equipment and surfaces. If you choose to use your own staff, be sure to have the equipment or surfacing manufacturer's representative witness or direct the installation. If you do not, and it is proven the installation does not comply with the manufacturer's specifications, your program will be liable for accidents caused by failures of the equipment and surfacing.

Another, and recently more popular, approach to installation is assembling a crew of community volunteers to build a playground and install equipment and surfacing, often over one long weekend. This has much to recommend it: civic pride, community involvement, and ownership of the playground. At the same time, this approach presents challenges that professional installation does not, most notably coordinating laypeople who may know little or nothing about construction but who must nonetheless adhere to the standards or guidelines of manufacturers, as well as those of CPSC, ASTM International, and the ADA. Because of its value in building community involvement and its increasing popularity, this method of installation is often worth the extra effort your staff must put into it.

Community installation may present additional challenges to you and your program. First, you must ensure that your organization and each volunteer is covered by your liability insurance during installation (if volunteers are not covered, their own home owner's insurance may cover them, but you should not depend on this as a fallback). Second, a manufacturer's or distributor's representative should be present to verify that volunteers follow all installation instructions. Third, your installation timeline will need to reflect the schedules of volunteers: while you may plan for a whirlwind weekend installation, inclement weather, poor turnout, or other unforeseen complications may delay work, and the project may need to fall back to much slower weekday or evening installation. During these delays, you must prevent children from using the dangerous, partly constructed play areas.

Signing Off

Your carefully planned and executed playground is finished, and it is beautiful and SAFE! Here is how to wrap up the project, dotting the last i and crossing that last t.

Manufacturer's Sign-Off

No matter who performed the actual installation, make sure the manufacturer's representative signs off on each piece of equipment and surfacing, stating that each item was installed according to specifications. Place the sign-offs in a permanent file.

Safety Auditor's Sign-Off

A neutral third party should conduct a comprehensive, first-time **safety audit** of all playground equipment, structures, and surfacing based on current CPSC guidelines and ASTM International standards. This will establish your baseline for future maintenance. The audit should identify all structures and surfacing on the playground, describe their condition, and assess their conformity to current guidelines and standards. Place the audit in a permanent file.

Congratulations on a job well done and a playground SAFE for the children entrusted to your care!

Discussion Questions

1. Exchange imaginary playground sites and age range of the children who will use them with a classmate or colleague; these sites can be empty ones or ones that presently have structures on them. Then do an on-site assessment of the space you have been given for its suitability as a playground for children of the age range you have been given. Consider nearby traffic, hazards, grade of ground, shade patterns, and other relevant factors.
2. How many people, representing what kind of experience, would you want to become planning committee members for your imaginary playground? Why?

List of Appendixes

Appendix A: SAFE Supervisory Checklist

Appendix B: Sample Injury Report Form for Playground Injuries

Appendix C: ADA Accessibility Checklist

Appendix D: State Regulations

Appendix E: Fall Heights for Equipment

Appendix F: Playground Use Zone Guidelines for Equipment

Appendix G: Routine Safety and Maintenance Inspection Checklists

Appendix H: Sample Documentation Records

SAFE Supervisory Checklist

Use this checklist to determine whether a play area is safe for children who will be playing there under your supervision.

1. Y ☐ N ☐ N/A ☐   Are you prepared to supervise your children at the playground?

2. Y ☐ N ☐ N/A ☐   Is there age-appropriate equipment for the children to play on?

3. Y ☐ N ☐ N/A ☐   Is the equipment in good condition?

4. Y ☐ N ☐ N/A ☐   Is the equipment located away from high-traffic areas, ponds, and parking lots?

5. Y ☐ N ☐ N/A ☐   Does the play area have appropriate surfacing materials?

6. Y ☐ N ☐ N/A ☐   Are all spaces and gaps less than 3.5 inches (9 cm.) wide or greater than 9 inches (23 cm.) wide to prevent head entrapments?

7. Y ☐ N ☐ N/A ☐   Are all spaces and gaps closed?

8. Y ☐ N ☐ N/A ☐   Are surfaces on all equipment smooth?

9. Y ☐ N ☐ N/A ☐   Are surfaces on all equipment cool enough to touch safely?

10. Y ☐ N ☐ N/A ☐   Is the play area clean and free of trash and other foreign objects?

11. Y ☐ N ☐ N/A ☐   _____

12. Y ☐ N ☐ N/A ☐   _____

13. Y ☐ N ☐ N/A ☐   _____

14. Y ☐ N ☐ N/A ☐   _____

Sample Injury Report Form
for Playground Injuries

1. Student's name: _____

2. School name: _____

3. Grade: _____

4. Date of injury: _____

5. ( ) Male ( ) Female

6. Time of injury: _____

7. Days absent: ____ Less than ½ ____ ½ ____ 1 ____ 1½–2 ____ 2½–3 ____
Other: _____

8. First aid given:

_____ Iced	_____ Washed wound	_____ Kept immobile
_____ Observed	_____ Stopped bleeding	_____ Applied splint
	_____ Applied dressing	_____ Other

Explain: _____

9. Body part injured:

Head	**Trunk**	**Extremities**	**Other**
___ Ear	___ Abdomen	___ Ankle	___ Lower arm
___ Eye	___ Back	___ Elbow	___ Lower leg
___ Face	___ Chest	___ Finger	___ Thumb
___ Head	___ Groin	___ Foot	___ Toes
___ Neck	___ Shoulder	___ Hand	___ Upper arm
___ Scalp	___ Trunk	___ Hip	___ Upper leg
		___ Knee	___ Wrist

10. Type of injury suspected:

_____ Laceration/abrasion   _____ Bruise/contusion   _____ Sprain/strain

_____ Dislocation   _____ Fracture   _____ Concussion

_____ Surface cut/Scratch   _____ Burn   _____ Other:

11. Action taken:

_____ Returned to class _____ Parent took home _____ Parent took to doctor

_____ Parent took to ER _____ Called 911   _____ Transfer to hospital

_____ Other: _____

_____ Time spent in nurse's office

12. Explanation of accident:

_____ Collision with person   _____ Collision with obstacle

_____ Hit with object   _____ Injury to self

_____ Fall   _____ Height of fall

Other: _____

13. Accident location:

_____ Classroom   _____ Playground   _____ Gym   _____ Assembly

_____ Stairs   _____ Hallway   _____ Bus   _____P.E. class

Time of accident:

_____ Before school   _____ After school   Other: _____

14. Surface:

_____ Blacktop   ____ Dirt   _____ Grass   ____ Synthetic surface

_____ Carpet   ____ Pea gravel ____ Mats   ____ Rubber tile

_____ Concrete   ____ Ice/snow   ____ Sand   ____ Wood products

Other: _____

15. Activity:

Baseball/softball	Basketball	Bicycling
Climbing	Dodgeball	Fighting
Flag/touch football	Jumping	Kickball
Playing on bars	Playground equipment	Roughhousing
Running	Sliding	Sliding on ice
Soccer	Snowballs	Swinging
Throwing rocks	Track/field	Volleyball
Walking		

Other: _____

16. Equipment:

Was playground equipment involved in injury?   ___ Yes ___ No

If yes, (a) Did equipment appear to be used appropriately?   ___ Yes ___ No

     (b) Was there any apparent malfunction of equipment?   ___ Yes ___ No

On which piece of equipment did the injury occur?

___ Arch climber	___ Slide	___ Cargo net
___ Swing	___ Chinning bar	___ Track ride
___ Horizontal ladder	___ Seesaw	___ Other

17. Describe specifically how the injury happened:

_____

_____

_____

_____

Signed: _____   Signed: _____

    (Person filing report)   (Principal)

Instructions for Filling Out the Form

This form is to be completed immediately following the occurrence of any injury that is severe enough to do the following:

    a. cause the loss of one-half day or more of school,

    b. warrant medical attention and treatment (i.e., school nurse, MD, ER),

    c. and/or require reporting according to school district policy.

Below is a breakdown of steps and additional information relating to each number in the Sample Injury Report Form.

Number	Description of Each Number
1–6	Self-explanatory.
7	Do not file a form until you have filled in days missed. If student is going to be absent for an extended period of time, use parent's estimate. If no school is missed, check "Less than ½".
8–11	Self-explanatory. Record the amount of time child was in the nurse's office. Please include "h" for hours and "m" for minutes (for example, 1h:40m).
12	*Collision with person* includes injuries that result from interactions between players from incidental or intended contact. *Hit with object* includes incidents involving an object (ball, backpack, etc). *Collision with obstacle* includes contact when the child collides with an object (playground equipment, fence, etc.). *Injury to self* occurs when a child got injured because of an action he/she carried out. *Fall* injuries are those when the student falls from equipment or falls while running. *Height of fall*. Report the height from where the child fell.
13	Self-explanatory.
14	Describe surface over which injury occurred.
15	Circle the activity the child was doing when he/she got injured.
16	Self-explanatory.
17	Briefly describe specifically how the incident happened. Make sure to include all names of witnesses present. If additional space is needed, continue on another sheet of paper and attach.

Appendix C

ADA Accessibility Checklist

Use this checklist to ensure your playground is ADA compliant:

1. The play area has an accessible route that enables a child to move from the edge of the play area to equipment.   Yes   No

2. The accessible route has acceptable materials for surfacing.   Yes   No

3. Number of ground-level play components _____

    Type of ground-level play components _____

4. Number of Elevated play components _____

5. Number of ground-level play components _____ to elevated play components _____

    Is ratio in compliance?   Yes   No

6. Based on number 4, are ramps a requirement? (More than 20 elevated)   Yes   No

    (a) If yes, are ramps provided?   Yes   No

7. Is a transfer system present for elevated structures under 20 in number?   Yes   No

8. Is space for wheelchair maneuvering to and from the play component provided?   Yes   No

9. Is parking space available for a wheelchair at the play component?   Yes   No

10. Is sufficient height and clearance present at play tables to accommodate wheelchairs?   Yes   No

11. Is the height of entry points or seats appropriate?   Yes   No

12. Are transfer supports available?   Yes   No

From *SAFE and Fun Playgrounds: A Handbook* by Heather M. Olsen, EdD, Susan D. Hudson, PhD, and Donna Thompson, PhD, © 2016. Published by Redleaf Press, www.redleafpress.org.

Appendix D

State Regulations

The key to successful advocacy is persistence. Ongoing follow-up is needed to ensure that old playgrounds get audited and renovated and that new playgrounds meet the current safety requirements. Getting a law passed is a great first step—and a big one. Then it will take continued, active advocacy to ensure that the necessary safety inspections take place and that funds will be made available to make playgrounds as safe as possible.

At the state level, lawmakers—often urged by consumers—have passed legislation or regulations addressing playground safety in fifteen states, with a wide range of requirements. The strongest regulations require all public playgrounds in the state to comply with the CPSC guidelines, and sometimes also ASTM International standards. The weakest regulations narrowly focus only on child care settings. These weak regulations require compliance with CPSC guidelines for protective surfacing only, suggesting only consultation with CPSC guidelines for other areas, or providing playground safety in a list of potential courses for day care providers.

Arkansas

The Arkansas Department of Education Rules and Regulations Governing Arkansas Better Chance Program Regulations (Code Ark. R. 005 24 001) sets the general guidelines for the operation of early childhood programs funded under the Arkansas Better Chance Program. In section 13.13, the regulation outlines that outdoor play areas should be developmentally appropriate and meet the CPSC requirements for child care facilities (Ark Code Ann. § 20-78-201-20 and the Child Care Facility Licensing Act, Act 434 of 1969, as amended) also require that all equipment installed on or after September 1, 1997, which is designed to be permanently anchored, must meet and be installed according to CPSC standards that are in effect at the time (Section 902[2] and 802[1] respectively).

California

The California Health and Safety Code (115725) was the first state legislation to mandate development of comprehensive statewide regulations for playground safety, requiring adoption of such regulations by January 1, 1992. The statewide regulations are required to be at least as protective as the CPSC guidelines. They also must include special provisions for child care settings and address the needs of the developmentally disabled. After the effective date of these regulations, no state funds may be used for the planning, development, or redevelopment of a playground unless the playground conforms to the regulations. In addition, all public agencies must specifically upgrade their playgrounds by replacement or improvement as necessary to satisfy the regulations (115730).

Until recently, however, no regulations had been enacted. Title 22, "Safety Regulations for Playgrounds" of the California Code of Regulation, was filed on December 12, 1999, and went into effect on January 1, 2000. These statewide regulations provide detailed specifications for the design, installation, and maintenance of public playgrounds, referencing compliance with CPSC and ASTM International guidelines as mandatory. In addition, operators of public playgrounds are required to have an initial inspection of their playgrounds by a Certified Playground Safety Inspector by October 1, 2000; then upgrades must be made to satisfy the regulations as required by the previous noted code provisions.

Connecticut

Connecticut's Department of Consumer Protection (Title 21a, Chapter 416, Section 21a–12a) required the development of a training and educational program on playground safety issues, as well as the adoption of standards for playground safety issues and the adoption of standards for playground equipment. The state subsequently adopted CPSC guidelines—as voluntary rather than mandatory—with an effective date of January 1, 1997, and made the annual presentation of a training and education program merely permissive rather than required.

Florida

Florida's Child Care Standards (F.A.C. 65C-22.003) include playground safety in the list of potential courses required to be taken by child care providers.

Illinois

Illinois's licensing standards for day care centers (89 Ill. Adm. Code 407.390) set forth requirements for playground equipment at those locations. The standards require that protective surfacing be in compliance with CPSC guidelines. Other components of the standards do not specifically mandate compliance with CPSC guidelines, but instead outline similar requirements. For example, the Illinois law requires that there be a 6-foot (1.8 m.) fall zone around all equipment, except swings. The fall zone for swings must extend both forward and backward a distance of at least two times the height measured from the supporting bar. In addition, swing seats are to be made of rubber or impact-absorbing material and have an impact-absorbing design. Standards are included to prevent entrapment hazards such that no openings between 3.5 and 9 inches (8.9 and 22.9 cm.) shall exist. In addition, daily inspection of the playground is required by a day care director or designee before children go out to play, in order to ensure no hazards are present.

Michigan

Laws in Michigan require all new playground equipment to satisfy both CPSC and ASTM International specifications, effective September 1, 1997. The laws also impose state civil penalties on those who violate these specifications for manufacturing or assembling playground equipment.

New Jersey

New Jersey enacted a playground safety law on March 23, 1999, to require that the Department of Community Affairs and Department of Education promulgate rules and regulations for the design, installation, inspection, and maintenance of playgrounds. This law also mandates that those rules and regulations be those contained within the CPSC guidelines. Further, it requires that special provisions be included to address playgrounds appropriate for children in child care settings. Government entities and private entities must upgrade their playgrounds to satisfy the rules and regulations for surfacing within five years and for all other elements within eight years. Nonprofit entities must upgrade their playgrounds to satisfy the rules and regulations for surfacing within five years and for all other elements within fifteen years. All playgrounds built more than six months after the effective date of the rules and regulations must conform to those rules and regulations. New Jersey Public Interest Research Group (NJPIRG) was instrumental in achieving this statewide mandate.

North Carolina

North Carolina addresses playground safety for child care facilities by requiring all new equipment and surfacing to conform to CPSC guidelines beginning on January 1, 1996. Playground equipment and surfacing installed in child care facilities prior to January 1, 1996, must conform to CPSC guidelines by January 1, 1999. These state requirements also prohibit the use of gravel for surfacing if the area will serve children less than three years of age.

Oklahoma

The Oklahoma Administrative Code includes standards for playgrounds in child care settings as part of its licensing standards (O.A.C. 340:110-3-22). The standards make no mention of CPSC guidelines; rather, the standards set out, for the most part, weaker requirements than CPSC and ASTM International. For example, the regulations maintain that grass is an acceptable surface under equipment less than 4 feet (1.2 m.) high (340:110-3-22[b] [2] [B]), and that 6 inches (15.2 cm.) of loose-fill material is sufficient for adequate protective surfacing (340: 110-3-22[b] [4]). The regulations set out standards for fall zones of at least 6 feet (1.8 m.) for all equipment except swings, which require a fall zone distance twice the length of the swing's chain. The regulations also include entrapment and entanglement hazard prevention, as well as swing seat composition requirements.

Oregon

Oregon's administrative rules certifying the physical setting of child care settings (Or. Admin. R. 414-300-0150) require that the protective surfacing in child care center playgrounds must comply with the standards of the CPSC.

Rhode Island

Following a statewide audit of municipal playgrounds by the Department of Health, personnel in local parks and recreation received education and training to improve playgrounds. Space bond money was allocated to remove old, dangerous equipment and install new, safer playgrounds.

In addition, in December 1999, Rhode Island's Rules and Regulations for School Health Programs (R16-SCHO, Section 35) were amended to require that all public school playground equipment and surfaces meet current CPSC safety guidelines by July 1, 2002. To ensure school officials understood the new rules and regulations and how to implement them, the Department of Education provided a statewide workshop.

Tennessee

Tennessee's Licensure Rules for Child Care Centers Serving Pre-School Children (Tenn. Comp. R. & Regs. 1240-4-3-.08) include that the CPSC's *Public Playground Safety Handbook* or a similar authority be used for guidance on playground construction and maintenance. While consultation with the guidelines is suggested, compliance with the guidelines is not required. In fact, Tennessee rules explicitly state that fall zones should be between 4 and 6 feet (1.2 and 1.8 m.). This is not in compliance with CPSC guidelines, which require a minimum of 6 feet (1.8 m.). However, the Tennessee rules for playground surfacing do require that surfacing type and depth be in compliance with CPSC's guidelines.

Texas

The Texas Health & Safety Code (756.061) requires substantial compliance with the CPSC guidelines for the purchase and installation of new playground equipment and surfacing beginning on September 1, 1997, if public funds are used.

Utah

The administrative rules setting forth standards for child care center licensing (Utah Admin. R. 430-60) require that the protective surfacing in child care center playgrounds must comply with CPSC and ASTM International guidelines.

The rules also require a fall zone of 6 feet (1.8 m.) surrounding all playground equipment.

Virginia

The Minimum Standards for Licensed Child Day Centers for Virginia (22 VAC 15-30-310) require that a center develop written playground safety procedures, which must include provision for active supervision by staff and a method of maintaining resilient surfacing.

Appendix E

Fall Heights for Equipment

EQUIPMENT	FALL HEIGHT
Climbers—Preschool/School-Age	The distance between the highest part of the climbing component and the protective surfacing beneath it.
Climbers—Under Two	The maximum fall height for freestanding and composite climbing structures should be 32 inches (81.3 cm).
Sliding Poles Accessed from Platforms	The distance between the platform and the protective surface beneath it.
Sliding Poles Not Accessed from Platforms	The distance between a point 60 inches (152.4 cm) below the highest point of the pole and the protective surface.
Track Rides	The distance between the maximum height of the equipment and the protective surface beneath it.
Log Rolls	The distance between the highest portion of the rolling log and the protective surfacing beneath it.
Merry-Go-Rounds	The distance between the perimeter of the platform where the child could sit or stand and the protective surfacing beneath it.
Seesaws	The distance between the highest point any part of the seesaw can reach and the protective surfacing beneath it.
Slides	The distance between the transition platform and the protective surfacing beneath it.
Spring Rockers	The distance between whichever is higher: (1) the playing surface or (2) the seat, and the protective surfacing beneath it.
Swings	The vertical distance between the pivot point and the protective surfacing beneath it.
Other Equipment Not Specified	The distance between the highest designated play surface and the protective surface beneath it.

Appendix F

Playground Use Zone Guidelines for Equipment

EQUIPMENT	USE ZONE REQUIREMENTS
Stationary Equipment (Such as Stand-Alone Climbers, Merry-Go-Rounds, Spring Rockers, and Seesaws)	The use zone should extend a minimum of 6 feet (1.8 m.) in all directions from the perimeter of the equipment. Stationary equipment may overlap with neighboring equipment if there is at least 6 feet (1.8 m.) between equipment when adjacent designated play surfaces are no more than 30 inches (76.2 cm.) high or if there is at least 9 feet (2.7 m.) between equipment when adjacent designated play surfaces are more than 30 inches (76.2 cm.) high (CPSC 5.3.2.1.4).
Slides: Toddlers	In a limited-access environment, the use zone should be at least 3 feet (0.9 m.) around the perimeter of the slide. The area at the end of the slide should not overlap the use zone for any other equipment. In public areas with unlimited access, a standalone slide should have a use zone of at least 6 feet (1.8 m.) around the perimeter. For slides that are part of a composite structure, the minimum use zone between access components and the slide chute should be 3 feet (0.9 m.), with at least 6 feet (1.8 m.) from the end of the slide (CPSC 5.3.6.5).
Slides: Preschool, School-Age	The use zone in front of the access and to the sides of a slide should extend a minimum of 6 feet (1.8 m.) from the perimeter of the equipment. This recommendation does not apply to embankment slides or slides that are part of a composite structure. The use zone in front of the exit of a slide should never overlap the use zone of any other equipment; however, two or more slide use zones may overlap if their sliding paths are parallel. For slides less than or equal to 6 feet (1.8 m.) high, the use zone in front of the exit should be at least 6 feet (1.8 m.). For slides greater than 6 feet (1.8 m.) high, the use zone in front of the exit should be at least as long as the slide is high, up to a maximum of 8 feet (2.4 m.) (CPSC 5.3.6.5).

EQUIPMENT	USE ZONE REQUIREMENTS
Swings: Single-Axis, Bucket	The use zone for a full bucket swing should extend to the front and rear a minimum of twice the vertical distance from the top of the occupant's sitting surface to the pivot point. The use zone in front of and behind swings should never overlap with any other use zone. The use zone to the sides should extend a minimum of 6 feet (1.8 m.) from the perimeter of the swing. This 6-foot (1.8 m.) zone may overlap that of an adjacent swing structure or other playground equipment structure (CPSC 5.3.8.4).
Swings: Single-Axis, Belt	The use zone to the front and rear of single-axis swings should never overlap the use zone of another piece of equipment. The use zone in front of and behind the swing should be greater than to the sides of such swing since children may deliberately attempt to exit from a single-axis swing while it is in motion. The use zone for a belt swing should extend to the front and rear of a single-axis swing a minimum distance of twice the vertical distance from the pivot point and the top of the protective surface beneath it. The use zone to the sides of a single-axis swing should extend a minimum of 6 feet (1.8 m.) from the perimeter of the swing. This 6-foot (1.8 m.) use zone may overlap that of an adjacent swing structure or other playground equipment structure (CPSC 5.3.8).
Swings: Multi-Axis	The use zone should extend in any direction from a point directly beneath the pivot point for a minimum distance of 6 feet (1.8 m.) plus the length of the suspending members. This use zone should never overlap the use zone of any other equipment (CPSC 5.3.8.4.1).

Appendix G

Routine Safety and Maintenance Inspection Checklists

This appendix contains three comprehensive routine checklists that can be used to assess the safety of a play area and identify items that need maintenance or repair.

- SAFE Checklist: Playground Report Card—Use this general checklist to evaluate your play area and see if it makes the grade.
- SAFE Checklist: Daily Maintenance Quick Check—Use this frequently to identify maintenance needs resulting from recent use, abuse, or environmental conditions.
- SAFE Checklist: Caregiver Quick Check—Use this to determine whether a play area is safe for children under your care.

You can customize the checklists to include items or issues specific to your particular play area. Use the numbered blank lines to add simple checks, and use the back of the page to sketch a diagram of the area, mark hazards, draw sight lines, and so on.

SAFE Checklist: Playground Report Card

Use this checklist to evaluate your play area and give it a SAFE grade, which will help to determine whether improvements are needed.

Supervision

Y ☐ N ☐ *Adults present when children are on equipment.*

Y ☐ N ☐ Children can be easily viewed on equipment.

Y ☐ N ☐ Children can be viewed in crawl spaces.

Y ☐ N ☐ Rules are posted regarding expected behavior.

Age-Appropriate Design

Y ☐ N ☐ *Playground has separate areas for ages 6–23 months, 2–5 years, and 5–12 years.*

Y ☐ N ☐ Signage indicating age group for equipment provided.

Y ☐ N ☐ *Platforms have appropriate guardrails.*

Y ☐ N ☐ Platforms allow change of directions to get on/off structure.

Y ☐ N ☐ Equipment design prevents climbing outside the structure.

Y ☐ N ☐ Supporting structure prevents climbing on it.

Fall Surfacing

Y ☐ N ☐ *Suitable surfacing materials provided.*

Y ☐ N ☐ *Height of all equipment is 8 feet or lower.*

Y ☐ N ☐ *Appropriate depth of loose fill provided.*

Y ☐ N ☐ *6 foot use zone has appropriate surfacing.*

Y ☐ N ☐ *Concrete footings are covered.*

Y ☐ N ☐ Surface is free of foreign objects.

Equipment Maintenance

Y ☐ N ☐   *Equipment is free of noticeable gaps.*

Y ☐ N ☐   *Equipment is free of head entrapments.*

Y ☐ N ☐   *Equipment is free of broken parts.*

Y ☐ N ☐   *Equipment is free of missing parts.*

Y ☐ N ☐   Equipment is free of protruding bolts.

Y ☐ N ☐   Equipment is free of rust.

Y ☐ N ☐   Equipment is free of splinters.

Y ☐ N ☐   Equipment is free of cracks/holes.

*If any of the asterisked criteria are marked "No," the potential of a life-threatening injury is significantly increased.

Scoring System

Total the number of "Yes" answers and find your corresponding grade below.

20–24 = A: Congratulations on having a SAFE playground! Please continue to maintain this excellence.

17–19 = B: Your playground is on the way to providing a safe environment for children. Work on the areas checked "no."

13–16 = C: Your playground is potentially hazardous for children. Start to make improvements.

8–12 = D: Children are at risk on this playground. Take corrective measures.

0–7 = F: Do not allow children on this playground. Make changes immediately.

SAFE Checklist: Daily Maintenance Quick Check

Use this checklist daily or frequently to inspect the play area and identify maintenance needs resulting from recent use, abuse, or environmental conditions. Simply walk through the area and observe the general conditions.

1. Y ☐ N ☐ N/A ☐ Is all equipment free of damage resulting from vandalism such as graffiti, broken glass, trash, and so on?
2. Y ☐ N ☐ N/A ☐ Does each piece of equipment have all of its parts?
3. Y ☐ N ☐ N/A ☐ Are all parts on each piece of equipment still tight and secure?
4. Y ☐ N ☐ N/A ☐ Is all equipment free of exposed footers?
5. Y ☐ N ☐ N/A ☐ Is all wooden equipment intact, with no splitting or splintering?
6. Y ☐ N ☐ N/A ☐ Do swing chains hang freely, without being kinked, twisted, or wrapped around the top rail?
7. Y ☐ N ☐ N/A ☐ Are swing seats intact, with no splitting or cracking?
8. Y ☐ N ☐ N/A ☐ Is the climber free of wear and deterioration?
9. Y ☐ N ☐ N/A ☐ Is the surfacing material free of trash and other foreign objects?
10. Y ☐ N ☐ N/A ☐ Is the general area free of trash and other foreign objects?
11. Y ☐ N ☐ N/A ☐ Are walkways, steps, and platforms free of trash and other foreign objects?
12. Y ☐ N ☐ N/A ☐ Have trash cans been emptied?
13. Y ☐ N ☐ N/A ☐ Is the general area free of standing water?
14. Y ☐ N ☐ N/A ☐ Are restrooms and water fountains clean and functional?
15. Y ☐ N ☐ N/A ☐ _____
16. Y ☐ N ☐ N/A ☐ _____
17. Y ☐ N ☐ N/A ☐ _____
18. Y ☐ N ☐ N/A ☐ _____

SAFE Checklist: Caregiver Quick Check

Parents, guardians, and other adults should use this checklist to determine whether a play area is safe for children under their care.

1. Y □ N □ N/A □ Are you prepared to supervise your children at this playground?

2. Y □ N □ N/A □ Is there age-appropriate equipment for the children to play on?

3. Y □ N □ N/A □ Is the equipment in good condition?

4. Y □ N □ N/A □ Is the equipment located away from high traffic areas, ponds, and parking lots?

5. Y □ N □ N/A □ Does the play area have appropriate surfacing materials?

6. Y □ N □ N/A □ Are all spaces and gaps less than 3.5 inches (9 cm.) wide or greater than 9 inches (23 cm.) wide to prevent head entrapment?

7. Y □ N □ N/A □ Are all spaces and gaps closed?

8. Y □ N □ N/A □ Are surfaces on all equipment smooth?

9. Y □ N □ N/A □ Are surfaces on all equipment cool enough to touch safely?

10. Y □ N □ N/A □ Is the play area clean and free of trash and other foreign objects?

11. Y □ N □ N/A □ _____

12. Y □ N □ N/A □ _____

13. Y □ N □ N/A □ _____

14. Y □ N □ N/A □ _____

From *SAFE and Fun Playgrounds: A Handbook* by Heather M. Olsen, EdD, Susan D. Hudson, PhD, and Donna Thompson, PhD, © 2016. Published by Redleaf Press, www.redleafpress.org.

Appendix H

Sample Documentation Records

For each play area under your jurisdiction, document and keep a record of the following general information.

Document	Date Filed	Comments
GENERAL INFORMATION		
Planning meeting minutes		
Initial letters for bid		
Acceptance contract		
Invoice		
Equipment warranty		
Site plan/construction dates		
Itemized list and quantity of play components		
Parts list		
Initial safety audit		
Inspection history checklists		
Remedial action history (work orders)		
Incident reports (injury, vandalism)		
Other		
Other		

For each play area under your jurisdiction, document and keep a record of the following manufacturer information.

Document	Date Filed	Comments
MANUFACTURER'S INFORMATION		
Contact information		
Correspondence with manufacturer		
Manufacturer's compliance letters (certificates for ASTM International, CPSC, IPEMA)		
Manufacturer's installation drawings and instructions		
Manufacturer's installation verification		
Other		
Other		

From *SAFE and Fun Playgrounds: A Handbook* by Heather M. Olsen, EdD, Susan D. Hudson, PhD, and Donna Thompson, PhD, © 2016. Published by Redleaf Press, www.redleafpress.org.

Glossary

Definitions provided here are specific to safe playgrounds for children.

activity analysis. Study undertaken to ensure that activity centers have the resources needed to provide SAFE play. Should describe the activity, profile users, list needed resources and facilities, and specify required supports.

activity center. Area dedicated to a specific play activity—for example, nature, dramatic play, climbing.

age-appropriate design. Design incorporating developmentally appropriate challenges that also minimize risks.

ASTM International. Professional engineering organization, founded in 1898, which has developed widely adopted, voluntary standards for playground surfacing and equipment. Until 2001 it was known as the American Society for Testing and Materials (ASTM).

bubble format. Graphic symbols used to lay out a playground during the design phase; each bubble represents an activity center and needed equipment. Bubbles can overlap.

challenges. On playgrounds, equipment and activities that engage children's courage, gross-motor skills, and coordination, even when children may not be aware that they possess these abilities.

community installation. Volunteer-driven building and installation of playgrounds and their equipment.

CPSC. The US Consumer Product Safety Commission, a federal entity created in 1972 as part of the federal Consumer Product Safety Act. Charged with protecting the public and developing uniform safety standards for consumer products.

deceleration. The slowing of movement (acceleration) over time; in the case of playground safety, the slowing of movement during a fall.

entanglement. Snaring or strangling as a result of drawstrings, jewelry, or other cordlike materials becoming stuck in or wound around protruding parts like S-rings or wedges on playground equipment.

entrapment. The encasing of feet, arms, heads, or clothing in openings of playground equipment, resulting in children's being unable to remove themselves.

fall height. The distance between the highest designated surface of a play structure and the fall surface below.

fall surface. A human-made surface created to decelerate and cushion falls from playground equipment.

gravity force (g). Acceleration in relation to free falls depends on the mass of the falling object or person. The g, or gravity force on earth, is designated as 1, or standard gravity. Gravity forces higher than 200 g (those resulting from the impact of playground accelerations and falls) can result in life-threatening head injuries. See also ***head injury criteria (HIC).***

guidelines. Voluntary and statutory recommendations regulating such things as playground supervision, surfaces, equipment, design, and equipment. See also ***standards.***

head injury criteria (HIC). A formula for estimating the effects of acceleration (movement) and its duration on head injuries during playground falls. A HIC of 1000 is likely to produce a roughly 17 percent chance of life-threatening injury to the brain. HICs with gravity forces below 200 usually do not involve severe brain injuries unless they are sustained.

impact attenuation. The capacity of surfacing to absorb the impact of falls.

impalement. Lacerations or worse caused by children's bodies being pierced by protruding parts on playground equipment or trees.

negligence. Failure of those charged with the well-being of others to discharge their responsibilities. In the case of children on playgrounds, programs, organizations, and individuals can be found guilty of negligence when they fail to provide adequate supervision of children or maintenance of playgrounds and equipment.

preventive maintenance. Regularly scheduled maintenance involving intensive examination of equipment and surfaces of a playground.

protective barriers. Walls, fences, and other equipment designed to protect children from hazards, to contain activities, or to separate activity areas.

proximate cause. In legal terms, the actual cause of damage or injury. For example, when damage or injury is proven to be the direct result of a supervisor's actions or inactions, negligence is said to be the proximate cause.

quality of use. The theory that people's behavior is affected by their perception of the orderliness (or not) of their surroundings. First introduced in Beverly Driver's book *Elements of Outdoor Recreation Planning* (1974) and since used to support high-quality maintenance of public places.

remedial maintenance. Maintenance undertaken in response to problems uncovered during routine maintenance.

routine maintenance. Regularly scheduled maintenance; does not involve intensive examination of equipment and areas.

SAFE. Acronym devised by the authors for the four foundations of safe playgrounds:
> **S**upervised by appropriate individuals
> **A**ge-appropriate in design and layout
> **F**all-surfacing that contains approved surfacing material
> **E**quipment maintenance

safety audit. Comprehensive assessment of all playground equipment, structures, surfacing, and supervision, based on current CPSC guidelines and ASTM standards.

site analysis. Study undertaken by the planning committee of a proposed site, including its soil and geology, drainage, slope, vegetation, climate- and weather-related factors, existing structures, nearby land use, hazardous conditions, and how these may affect the project's goals and children's play.

standards. voluntary and statutory specifications regulating matters like playground supervision, surfaces, equipment, design, and equipment. See also *guidelines*.

standard of care. Court-determined criteria required of early childhood programs, school districts, and community parks, usually based on recognized professional practices of local and state programs. These, in turn, are often based on principles developed by the National Association for the Education of Young Children (NAEYC), the National Park and Recreation Association, the National AfterSchool Association, state and federal departments of education, and the National Education Association.

succotash syndrome. Playground "design" characterized by uncoordinated play elements and equipment randomly placed.

supervision. Moral and legal responsibility of those charged with the well-being and productivity of others (in this case, children).

surfacing. Natural and artificial materials used to lessen the impact of falls on playgrounds.

unitary fill. Surfaces whose particles are bonded together—for example, rubber tiles or mats, poured urethane, and rubber.

universal design. Design that accommodates the needs and abilities of children across a wide spectrum of developmental ages, stages, and abilities.

use zone. Safety area under and around playground equipment; must be equipped with appropriate surfacing to lessen the impact of falls.

Resources

Administration for Children and Families

https://www.acf.hhs.gov

Administration on Children, Youth, and Families

http://www.acf.hhs.gov/programs/acyf

American Academy of Pediatrics

http://www.aap.org/en-us/Pages/Default.aspx

American Public Health Association

https://www.apha.org

Americans with Disabilities Act (ADA)

http://www.ada.gov/index.html

For play area guidelines, visit:

http://www.access-board.gov/guidelines-and-standards/buildings
-and-sites/about-the-ada-standards/ada-standards
/chapter-2-scoping-requirements#240%20Play%20Areas

ASTM International

http://www.astm.org

Consumer Product Safety Commission (CPSC)

http://www.cpsc.gov

Guidelines for playground safety can be found here:

http://www.cpsc.gov/en/Safety-Education/Safety-Guides/Sports-Fitness
-and-Recreation/Playground-Safety/

Public Playground Safety Handbook can be found here:

http://www.cpsc.gov/PageFiles/122149/325.pdf

**Early Childhood Environmental Rating Scales (ECERS) and Infant/Toddler
Environmental Rating Scale (ITERS)**

http://ers.fpg.unc.edu

International Playground Contractors Association

www.playground-contractors.org

National AfterSchool Association

http://naaweb.org

National Association for the Education of Young Children (NAEYC)

http://www.naeyc.org

National Education Association

http://www.nea.org

National Playground Safety Institute (NPSI)

www.nrpa.org

National Program for Playground Safety (NPPS)

http://www.playgroundsafety.org

National Recreation and Park Association

http://www.nrpa.org

National Resource Center for Health and Safety in Child Care and Early Education

http://nrckids.org

Office of Head Start

http://www.acf.hhs.gov/programs/ohs

State of Virginia

http://www.virginia.gov

US Department of Defense

http://www.defense.gov

US Department of Education

http://www.ed.gov

US Department of Health and Human Services

http://www.hhs.gov

References

American Academy of Pediatrics, American Public Health Association, and National Resource Center for Health and Safety in Child Care and Early Education. 2011. *Caring for Our Children: National Health and Safety Performance Standards: Guidelines for Early Care and Education Programs,* 3rd Ed. Elk Grove Village, IL: American Academy of Pediatrics; Washington DC: American Public Health Association.

ASTM International. 2011a. "F1487: Standard Consumer Safety Performance Specification for Playground Equipment for Public Use." *Book of Standards* 15.11. West Conshohocken, PA. doi:10.1520/F1487-11.

———. 2011a. "F2373: Standard Consumer Safety Performance Specification for Public Use Play Equipment for Children 6 Months through 23 Months." *Book of Standards* 15.11. West Conshohocken, PA. doi:10.1520/F2373-11.

———. 2013b. "F1292: Standard Specification for Impact Attenuation of Surfacing Materials within the Use Zone of Playground Equipment." *Book of Standards* 15.07. West Conshohocken, PA. doi:10.1520/F1292.

———. 2014. "F1951: Standard Specification for Determination of Accessibility of Surfacing Systems under and around Playground Equipment." *Book of Standards* 15.07. West Conshohocken, PA. doi:10.1520/F1951-14.

Bertenthal, Bennett I., Joseph J. Campos, and Karen Caplovitz Barrett. 1984. "Self-produced Locomotion: An Organizer of Emotional, Cognitive, and Social Development in Infancy." In *Continuities and Discontinuities in Development: Topics in Developmental Psychology*, edited by Robert N. Ernde and Robert J. Harmon, 175–220. New York: Plenum. doi:10.1007/978-1-4613-2725-7_8.

Brault, Matthew W. 2012. "Americans with Disabilities: 2010: Household Economics Studies." *Current Population Reports.* Washington, DC: US Census Bureau. Accessed May 12, 2015. www.census.gov/prod/2012pubs/p70-131.pdf.

Brown, V. R. 1978. *Human Factors Analysis of Injuries Associated with Public Playground Equipment.* Washington, DC: Consumer Product Safety Commission.

Campos, Joseph J., Bennett I. Bertenthal, and Rosanne Kermoian. 1992. "Early Experience and Emotional Development: The Emergence of Wariness of Heights." *American Psychology Society* 3, no. 1: 61–64.

CPSC (US Consumer Product Safety Commission). 2010. *Public Playground Safety Handbook.* Bethesda, MD.

DeMary, Jo Lynne, and A.K. Ramnarain. 2003. *From Playgrounds to Play/Learning Environments.* Richmond, VA: Commonwealth of Virginia Department of Education.

Dougherty, Neil, David Auxter, Alan Goldberger, and Greg Heinzmann. 1993. *Sport, Physical Activity, and the Law.* Champaign, IL: Human Kinetics.

Driver, Beverly L. 1974. *Elements of Outdoor Recreation Planning.* Ann Arbor: University of Michigan Press.

Frost, Joe L. 1992. *Play and Playscapes.* Albany, NY: Delmar.

Frost, Joe L., Pei-San Brown, John A. Sutterby, and Candra D. Thornton. 2004. *The Developmental Benefits of Playgrounds.* Olney, MD: Association for Childhood Education International.

Frost, Joe L., Sue C. Wortham, and Stuart Reifel. 2011. *Play and Child Development.* 4th ed. Upper Saddle River, NJ: Pearson.

Gottlieb, Gilbert. 1983. "The Psychobiological Approach to Development Issues." In *Handbook of Child Psychology*, edited by Paul H. Mussen, 1–26. 4th ed. New York: Wiley.

———. 1991. "Experiential Canalization of Behavioral Development: Theory." *Developmental Psychology* 27, no. 1: 4–13.

Harms, Thelma, Richard Clifford, and Debby Cryer. 2005. *Early Childhood Environment Rating Scale.* New York: Teachers College Press.

Harms, Thelma, Debby Cryer, and Richard Clifford. 2006. *Infant/Toddler Environment Rating Scale.* New York: Teachers College Press.

Hendy, Teresa. 2004. "The Nuts and Bolts of Playground Maintenance." In *The SAFE Playground Handbook*, edited by Susan Hudson, 77–86. Cedar Falls, IA: National Program for Playground Safety.

Hudson, Susan, and Keith Abraham. 2010. "Supervision." In *Management of Park and Recreation Agencies,* edited by M. Moischeck, 193–205. 3rd ed. Asburn, VA: National Recreation and Parks Association.

Hudson, Susan, Mickey Mack, and Donna Thompson. 2000. *How Safe Are America's Playgrounds? A National Profile of Childcare, School and Park Playgrounds.* Cedar Falls, IA: National Program for Playground Safety.

Hudson, Susan, Heather Olsen, R. Dieser, and Donna Thompson. 2009. *Planning Accessible Safe Playgrounds Using the Americans with Disabilities Act.* 2nd ed. National Program for Playground Safety. CD ROM.

Hudson, Susan, Heather Olsen, and Donna Thompson. 2004. *How Safe Are America's Playgrounds? A National Profile of Childcare, School, and Park Playgrounds: An Update.* Cedar Falls, IA: National Program for Playground Safety.

———. 2008. "An Investigation of School Playground Safety Practices as Reported by School Nurses." *Journal of School Nursing* 24, no. 3: 138–44.

Hudson, Susan, Heather Olsen, Donna Thompson, and Lawrence Bruya. 2010. *SAFE Outdoor Play Supervision Manual: Early Childhood Edition.* Cedar Falls, IA: National Program for Playground Safety.

Hudson, Susan, and Donna Thompson. 1999. "Reducing Risk in Playgrounds." In *Play in a Changing Society: Research, Risk and Application,* edited by March Guddemi, Tom Jambor, and Audrey Skrupskelis, 61. Little Rock, AK: Southern Early Childhood Association.

Hudson, Susan, Donna Thompson, and Heather Olsen. 2008a. *Building Playgrounds.* Cedar Falls, IA: National Program for Playground Safety.

Hudson, Susan, Donna Thompson, and Mickey Mack. 1999. *Selecting Playground Surface Materials.* Cedar Falls, IA: National Program for Playground Safety.

King, Steve. 1995. *A Study of Maintenance Procedures in 900 Parks Department.* Delano, MN: Unpublished (Landscape Structures).

Kitzes, William. 2001. "Standards, Regulations and Safety Guidelines to Protect Children from Injury." In *Children and Injuries,* edited by Joe Frost, 10–151. Tucson, AZ: Lawyers & Judges.

Knapp, Richard, and Charles Hartsoe. 1979. *Play for America, 1906–1965.* Arlington, VA: National Recreation and Parks Association.

Mero, Everett. 1908. *American Playgrounds: Their Construction, Equipment, Maintenance and Utility.* Boston: Dale Association.

Miller, Norman P., and Duane Morris Robinson. 1963. *The Leisure Age: It's Challenge to Recreation.* Belmont, CA: Wadsworth.

Moore, Robin C., Susan M. Goltsman, and Daniel S. Iacofano. 1987. *Play for All Guidelines: Planning, Design and Management of Outdoor Play Settings for All Children.* Berkeley: MIG Communications.

Morrongiello, Barbara A., and Stacey L. Schell. 2010. "Child Injury: The Role of Supervision in Prevention." *American Journal of Lifestyle Medicine* 4, no. 1 (2010): 65–74. doi:10.1177/1559827609348475

National Association for the Education of Young Children. 2014. *NAEYC Early Childhood Program Standards and Accreditation Critera & Guidance for Assessment.* http://www.naeyc.org/academy/files/academy/file/AllCriteriaDocument.pdf

National Electronic Injury Surveillance System. 2009. *Injury Report on Playground Incidents (1990–1999).* Washington, DC: US Consumer Product Safety Commission.

National Head Start Training and Technical Assistance Resource Center. *2005. Head Start Design Guide: A Guide for Building a Head Start Facility.* Arlington, VA: National Head Start Training and Technical Assistance Resource Center.

National Program for Playground Safety. 2000. *Building Playgrounds: A Guide to the Planning Process.* Cedar Falls, IA: National Program for Playground Safety.

National Recreation and Park Association (NRPA). 1976. *Proposed Safety Standard for Public Playground Equipment.* Arlington, VA.

———. 1992. *Playground Equipment for Public Use: Continuum of Skills and Size Differences of Children Age Two to Twelve.* Arlington, VA.

National Recreation Association (NRA). 1907. NRA board minutes, April 12, 1906. *Recreation,* 13–15. New York.

———. 1931. *Report of Committee on Standards in Playground Apparatus* (Bulletin 2170). New York.

O'Brien, Craig W. 2009. "Injuries and Investigated Deaths Associated with Playground Equipment, 2001–2008." Bethesda, MD: US Consumer Product Safety Commission. www.cpsc.gov/library/foia/foia10/os/playground.pdf.

Olsen, Heather, Susan Hudson, and Donna Thompson. 2003. "Strategies for Playground Injury Prevention: An Overview of a Playground Project." *American Journal of Health Education* 4, no. 3 (May–June): 187–92.

Playground and Recreation Association of America (PRAA). 1928. *Play Areas: Their Design and Equipment.* New York: Barnes.

Rudolph, Cuno, H. 1907. "Presidential Addresses and State Papers VI, 1163." Washington, DC: Washington Playground Association. February 16, 1907.

Saluja, Gitanjali, Ruth Brenner, Barbara A. Morrongiello, Denise Haynie, Michelle Rivera, and Tina L. Cheng. 2004. "The Role of Supervision in Child Injury Risk: Definition, Conceptual and Measurement Issues." *Injury Control and Safety Promotion* 11, no. 1:17–22.

Sawyer, Thomas H., ed. 2009. *Facility Planning and Design.* 12th ed. Champaign, IL: Sagamore.

Thompson, Donna, Susan Hudson, and Heather Olsen. 2007. *SAFE Play Areas: Creation, Maintenance, and Renovation.* Champaign, IL: Human Kinetics.

US Department of Defense. 2002. "Design: Child Development Centers." *Unified Facilities Criteria (UFC).* Washington, DC: US Department of Defense.

US Department of Health and Human Services. Head Start Bureau. 2009. Safety First: Preventing and Managing Childhood Injuries (p. 93). Accessed February 1, 2010. http://eclkc.ohs.acf.hhs.gov/hslc/resources/ECLKC_Bookstore/PDFs/Safety _First.pdf

US Department of Justice. 2010. "ADA Standards for Accessible Design: Play Areas." *Federal Register* (September 15, 2010). Washington, DC.

Van der Smissen, Betty. 1990. *Legal Liability and Risk Management for Public and Private Entities: Sport and Physical Education, Leisure Services, Recreation and Parks, Camping Adventure Activities.* Vol. 2. Cincinnati: Anderson.

———. 2007. "Elements of Negligence." In *Law for Recreation and Sport Managers,* edited by Doyice Cotton and John Wolohan, 36–45. 4th ed. Dubuque, IA: Kendall Hunt.

Wade, Michael G., M. J. Ellis, and M. E. Bohrer. 1973. "Biorhythms in the Activity of Children During Free Play." *Journal of the Experimental Analysis of Behavior* 20, no. 1: 155–62.

Warden, Claire. 2010. *Nature Kindergartens and Forest Schools.* Scotland: Mindstretchers LTD.

Wardle, Francis. 2008. "Play as Curriculum." *Earlychildhood NEWS: The Professional Resource for Teachers and Parents.* Accessed May 21, 2015. www.earlychildhoodnews. com/earlychildhood/article_view.aspx?ArticleId=127.

INDEX

Page numbers in *italics* represent figures; those in bold represent tables.